COURTESY MRS. J. AUSTIN DU PONT, TABLE NO. 247

MINIATURE ANTIQUE FURNITURE

By Herbert F. *and*
Peter B. Schiffer

LIVINGSTON PUBLISHING COMPANY
Wynnewood, Pennsylvania

Library of Congress Cataloging in Publication Data
Schiffer, Herbert F.   1917-
    Miniature antique furniture.

    1. Miniature furniture — United States — Catalogs.
I. Schiffer, Peter Berwind, joint author.   II. Title.
NK2750.S35   749.2   72-12679
ISBN 0-87098-049-1

TO

Mr. Theodore Kapnek, Sr. and Mrs. J. Austin duPont we dedicate this book. We are deeply indebted to these two kind and encouraging people who have not only answered our innumerable questions, but also have permitted us to upset their households, blow their fuses, and handle their treasured miniatures.

LIST OF OWNERS

Museums

Art Institute of Chicago
Michigan Avenue at Adams Street
Chicago, Illinois

Chester County Historical Society
225 North High Street
West Chester, Pennsylvania

Colonial Williamsburg, Inc.
Goodwin Building
Williamsburg, Virginia

Connecticut Historical Society
1 Elizabeth Street
Hartford, Connecticut

Germantown Historical Society
5214 Germantown Avenue
Philadelphia, Pennsylvania

Greenfield Village and Henry Ford Museum
Dearborn, Michigan

Metropolitan Museum of Art
Fifth Avenue at 82nd Street
New York, New York

Monmouth County Historical Association
70 Court Street
Freehold, New Jersey

Museum of Early Southern Decorative Arts
Salem Station
Winston-Salem, North Carolina

Museum of Fine Arts
Boston, Massachusetts

New Hampshire Historical Society
30 Park Street
Concord, New Hampshire

Old Salem Inc.
600 South Main Street
Winston-Salem, North Carolina

Old Sturbridge Village
Sturbridge, Massachusetts

Philadelphia Museum of Art
Benjamin Franklin Parkway at 26th Street
Philadelphia, Pennsylvania

Reich Museum
Amsterdam, Holland

Smithsonian Institution
Washington, D.C.

Upsula Foundation
6430 Germantown Avenue
Philadelphia, Pennsylvania

Victoria and Albert Museum
South Kensington
London S.W., England

Wadsworth Atheneum
25 Atheneum Square North
Hartford, Connecticut

William Penn Memorial Museum
Harrisburg, Pennsylvania

Henry Francis duPont Winterthur Museum
Winterthur, Delaware

Yale University Art Gallery
Chapel Street
New Haven, Connecticut

Private Collections

Mrs. Frederick Barbour
Mr. & Mrs. Ray Blake
Mr. & Mrs. Robert P. Butler
Mrs. Henry Clark
Mr. John Clifford
Mrs. Charles Dorman
Mrs. J. Austin duPont
Mr. & Mrs. H. C. Foster
C. Fredericks & Son
Miss Natalie Fredericks
Mr. Richard Fredericks
Mr. & Mrs. Robert Lee Gill
Mr. Philip Hammerslaugh
Mrs. E. M. Hartman
Mr. Peter Hill
Mr. Walter Himmelreich
Miss Elizabeth D. Horne
Mr. & Mrs. Theodore Kapnek

Dr. W. M. King
Mr. John Litten
Mr. & Mrs. Ken Litten
Mr. Philip Parker
Mr. & Mrs. Jess Pavey
Mrs. Carl B. Randall
Israel Sack, Inc.
Mrs. Herbert F. Schiffer
Herbert Schiffer Antiques
Mr. Peter B. Schiffer
Mr. David Stockwell
Mr. & Mrs. Stanley Stone
Mr. & Mrs. Edward V. Stvan
Mr. & Mrs. Laurent Jean Torno
R. T. Trump & Co., Inc.
John S. Walton, Inc.
Mr. Roger Warner
Mr. Simon M. Warner
Mr. & Mrs. Mead Willis, Jr.

ACKNOWLEDGMENTS

WHILE MANY HAVE HELPED and encouraged us during the preparation of this book, we acknowledge in particular the following people: Mr. Edward LaFond, who wrote the introduction to the clock section and selected the clocks; Mr. Eris deJonge at the William Penn Memorial Museum for much helpful advice and patience; Mr. H. R. Bradley Smith of the Shelburne Museum for suggestions and help; Dr. Donald Shelly and his able staff at the Henry Ford Museum for supplying some of our most interesting pictures and many suggestions; Mr. Bart Anderson for many ideas and editing; Mr. Travis Cox for allowing photography; Miss Dorothy Lapp for helping to select items at the Chester County Historical Society; Mrs. Nancy Goyne Evans for helping us to check measurements and details; Mrs. Karol A. Schmiegel, who answered many questions; and Dr. Frank Sommers for encouragement at The Henry Francis duPont Winterthur Museum.

We also thank Mr. John Evans of the Decorative Arts Photographic Collections; Mr. Berry B. Tracy for help at the Metropolitan Museum of Art; Mr. Paul Koda and Mr. Philip Hammerslaugh for help in finding and describing many Connecticut examples; and Mr. James Elliot of the Wadsworth Atheneum.

Also, help and encouragement was given by Mr. Frank Horton, Mr. John Bivins, Jr. and Mr. Bradford L. Rauschenburg of Old Salem, Inc.; Mr. Charles F. Montgomery of the Mabel Grady Garvan Collection at the Yale University Art Gallery for his encouragement; by Mr. Ray Shepherd at the Pennsylvania Museum of Art; and by Mrs. Edward Feltus at the Monmouth County Historical Association.

In addition, our thanks are extended to Mr. and Mrs. Herbert Foster and Messrs. Robert and Gailey Wilson for their help in locating examples of Western Pennsylvania inlaid miniatures; to Mr. John Snyder, Jr. of the University of Delaware for sharing his knowledge of the Lancaster school of cabinet work; to Miss Nancy Nutt at The Smithsonian Institution for her helpful research; to Mr. Robert Trump for his help with Philadelphia furniture; and to Miss Elizabeth M. Aslin for her time and trouble at the Victoria and Albert Museum and for permitting us to examine parts of the collection.

Much gratitude is due Mrs. Herbert Schiffer for proofreading and editorial help; Mr. John F. Lewis III for help on business and editorial matters; Mrs. Emma Garrett for many measurements and infinite details; and last, but not least, Mrs. George Drenker for typing, retyping and correcting this manuscript.

Our thanks also go to Mr. Douglass S. Livingston for his endless patience in explaining and helping us to understand the complexities of publishing this book, and to his long-suffering editor, Mrs. Susan M. Butler, for translating our technical jargon into English.

We appreciate the photographic accomplishments of Mr. Arthur Helga, who took some of the color pictures under very difficult circumstances; of Mr. Laurent Jean Torno, who provided such wonderful photographs; of Miss Dannielle Greenberg, who, during a heat wave, took many of the pictures, particularly those of Western Pennsylvania furniture; of Mr. Martin Schweig of St. Louis, Missouri, and of Mr. Douglas S. Faulkner, of our staff for their superb photographic work.

Most important, our sincere thanks are extended to the many kind people who fuses we blew and whose home we disrupted, while photographing their furniture.

With a deep sense of gratitude, we wish to thank again the owners and the staff of the public institutions for their repeated courtesies.

CONTENTS

MINIATURE
ANTIQUE FURNITURE

INTRODUCTION

D

EXAMPLE A, LATE 17th CENTURY DOLLS' HOUSE, REICH MUSEUM, AMSTERDAM

THIS BOOK IS INTENDED as a pictorial survey of a heretofore unpublished subject, children's, doll's and miniature antique furniture. A study of this scope seemed necessary for several reasons. Although almost all museum and private collections of antiques contain miniatures, many questions have constantly been asked of us concerning this subject. It is also important that we explain, and therefore dispel, some of the misconceptions surrounding miniature furniture. In our effort to make the photographs tell a story, only those miniatures which fit into a series or serve to show a slight difference in date, execution, and regional characteristics were chosen.

For the last three centuries many people in England, Holland and America have loved and collected miniature furniture. The finest miniatures were made in Holland during the seventeenth century as toys for the royalty. They continued to make wonderful miniatures in the eighteenth century, including Bombé examples, claw and ball footed lowboys, and serpentine chests of drawers. All of these are later forms and are not in the realm of this book, as by then the English and American examples were being pro-

EXAMPLE D, KITCHEN DETAIL

duced. We have included the earliest forms of Dutch furniture because they are not generally seen in English furniture, and are certainly too early to have existed among the American examples.

English miniatures dating before the Restoration are quite crude; one surmises that while Charles II was in exile in Holland, he and his court must have seen the exquisite miniature furniture. After the Restoration, England began to produce miniatures of excellent quality and, later, in large quantity.

The production and collection of miniature furniture was not the only form of amusement for the Dutch; high quality dollhouses were another popular conceit of the gentry. In the Reich Museum in Amsterdam, are two important dollhouses with interiors constructed in the late seventeenth century manner. Both dollhouses are great social documents. The first example shown here resembles a William and Mary cupboard-on-frame (Example B). When the doors are open the viewer sees a house interior (Example A). In the attic, in the left hand room, servants are hauling and stocking peat; maids are ironing and hanging linen in the center room; the room at the right is a nursery. The second floor is divided into two rooms in which there are several silver miniatures, Cromwellian chairs, and even a kas filled with household linen (Example C). The cellar contains a buttery, a delft-tiled kitchen (Example D), and an informal dining room.

EXAMPLE C   EXAMPLE B

17

EXAMPLE E, DOLLS' HOUSE *c.* 1700, REICH MUSEUM, AMSTERDAM

EXAMPLE F, ROOM DETAIL

The second dollhouse (Example E) exhibits a more realistic interior arrangement with its three floors, a flight of stairs and a hall. Refinements such as built-in shelves for Chinese export porcelain, flame stitch needlework hangings, and painted walls (Example F) make this dollhouse more sophisticated than the earlier example. Sleeping quarters for servants are on the third floor.

Almost two hundred years later in Philadelphia this next doll house was made by Voegler. It is now in the possession of the Chester County Historical Society. Few English or American dollhouses exist with their furniture intact. Most of the dollhouse furniture has been made during the last one hundred years. The rooms (Examples G, H, I, and J) in this dollhouse provide an excellent social commentary on the Philadelphia area during the nineteenth century. Almost all of the accessories and forms of furniture exist in standard form in the collections of the Chester County Historical Society.

G   H

I   J

An interesting dollhouse is displayed in England at Uppark near Petersfield. The Victoria and Albert Museum dollhouses and miniature furniture at the Bethnal Green Museum in London are worthy of a visit. For an excellent short study of this subject, we refer the reader to *Doll's Houses* published by the Victoria and Albert Museum.

Very few pieces of dollhouse furniture can be called antique. However, *Miniature Antique Furniture* discusses doll's furniture of known authenticity from Holland, England and the United States. Furniture is only one form of which miniatures were made. Many beautiful pieces of miniature silver, china, pictures and glass also exist. Many examples of miniature Dutch silver have survived, but English examples are rare. England did not produce any appreciable quantity of miniature porcelain or pottery until the time of Thomas Whieldon in the 1740s.

169

Misconceptions exist concerning the purpose and function of miniatures. Many believe miniatures were made to be used as salesman's samples, while others think they were made by apprentices to serve as masterpieces taking less material than their standard size counterparts. In reality, ninety-nine percent fall into neither category.

In the opinion of the late Joseph Kindig, Jr., one of the most knowledgeable and dynamic antique dealers whose working years covered almost the entire history of the collection and preservation of American furniture, there are almost no samples. Most miniatures were either children's playthings or trinkets for their parents' enjoyment. The one specimen which we feel was definitely made as a sample is very late. (No. 169.) It is certain that some miniatures were sold as toys. (See No. 194.)

102

21

In her study of over eleven thousand wills and inventories of Chester County, Mrs. Herbert F. Schiffer, author of *Furniture and Its Makers of Chester County, Pennsylvania* and *Historical Needlework of Pennsylvania,* has found no mention of miniatures. Yet, the Historical Society and collectors of Chester County furniture have assembled an important group of local miniatures. (See Nos. 21, 102, 103, and 138.) We find no reason why miniatures have not been mentioned in the wills and inventories. Unless they are referred to in some obscure manner in the inventories, it is probable that miniatures were considered common toys. This theory is supported by the fact that the inventories do not mention needlework which may have been considered of little value.

138

103

It is unlikely that miniatures were made as masterpieces. First, the labor involved in the production of a miniature is the same as that necessary to produce a standard size piece. Second, many miniatures were made to be looked at from above and, therefore, appear out of proportion when viewed from any other angle. A miniature requires as much time to repair as does a standard size piece of furniture. In a photograph, the best of miniature furniture can seldom be differentiated from standard scale furniture, unless there is something to indicate scale.

228

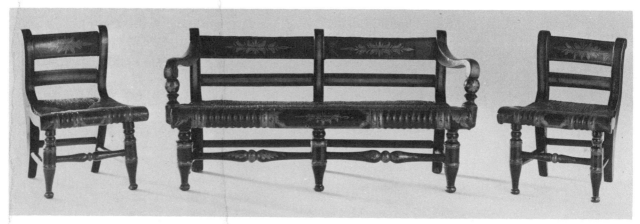

Miniatures were also made as doll's furniture. An elderly lady from Baltimore inherited, some years ago, two miniature chests of drawers—one a very small one, about 10″ tall, and other larger, about 22″ tall. By family tradition, the daughters in her family had always used these for their doll's clothes. This use is indicated in many of the inscriptions we have seen. (See No. 109.)

Miniature and children's furniture follows the style of standard size furniture. However, the style lags make dating miniature furniture more difficult. Note our No. 164; this fine court cupboard was made 200 years after the style was popular.

Many miniatures were made in sets. (See No. 228.) Some pieces are marked by a number to indicate they were part of a set. (See No. 52.) Some miniatures were obviously exact copies of standard size pieces. (Nos. 23 and 24.)

23   24

Another interesting feature is that, like many other fine types of cabinetwork, miniatures were often very regional in character and reflected the characteristics of a region to such an extent that, in some cases, they became caricatures. See Western Pennsylvania Nos. 114, 115, 116, 118, New England Nos. 142, 236, and Philadelphia Nos. 54, 136.

142

114

WESTERN PENNSYLVANIA

NEW ENGLAND

136

PHILADELPHIA

In general, miniatures seem to have been made during periods when particular regions were very prosperous and there was time for leisure and enjoyment. Some areas, such as Newport, produced few miniatures compared to Western Pennsylvania, the Connecticut Valley, and Philadelphia, which produced enormous quantities.

Why does one collect miniatures? It's a form of excitement to those who know antiques, and in a way, they are toys for grownups. Dealers, in particular, are avid collectors of miniatures. Since it would be difficult for a collector to keep all the standard size furniture he likes, he collects miniature versions of his favorites as an alternative. There is always room for "just one more" and few collectors are willing to part with their treasured miniatures at any price.

It has been very enjoyable examining the exquisite pieces of miniature furniture which have been incorporated into this survey. We sincerely hope that the reader will derive as much pleasure from the visual experience provided him by this book.

BEDS

1. DOLL'S PENCIL POST BED

H 13″ x W 9″ x L 28″
New England, *c.* 1720, Maple

The octagonal pencil posts on this doll's bed widen as they descend to join the bed rails, at which point they become square in section. The four extra sides terminate in lamb's-tongues above the juncture. Below the bed rails, which are pierced for ropes, the posts become octagonal again and remain so to the floor. The bed is held together by ropes, a construction detail found on the standard size beds of the period. The top edge of the headboard is scalloped and the tester has been restored. (For a standard size example, see Sack, *Fine Points of Furniture,* p. 90.)

Courtesy Herbert Schiffer Antiques

2. MINIATURE TALL POST BED

H 5¼″ x W 2½″ x L 4″
America, *c.* 1720, Poplar

This miniature pencil post bed which was made for a shell and wax works has its original drapery. The design of the drapery was used as a model for the drapery of a standard size bed in the restoration of the Brinton 1704 House. The posts are chamfered and the rails are pierced for rope.

Courtesy Chester County Historical Society

3

3. MINIATURE OR DOLL'S BED

H 50¾″ x W 12¾″ x L 22″
England, 1780-85, Mahogany

The most important aspect of this bed is its drapery which is made of the original period fabric and bears a revenue stamp of the period. Many restorations have used doll's bed draperies as a source of design. Note how fully this bed and bed No. 2 are draped. The draperies offered protection from drafts and provided warmth and privacy.

Courtesy Victoria and Albert Museum

4. MINIATURE DOLL'S BED

H 13½″ x W 8¾″ x L 12½″
America, 1790, Maple

This miniature bed's half-round tester is supported by four tall turned posts. Ring turnings and urns decorate the posts, which end in round spade feet, such as those found on some Connelly and Haines furniture made in Philadelphia. The bed rails are pierced for ropes which not only hold up the mattress, but also hold the bed together. The bed has a headboard, but no footboard. Doll's beds are one of the most commonly found pieces of miniature furniture.

Courtesy Metropolitan Museum of Art

5. CHILD'S HIGH POST BED

H (w/out tester) 54″ x H (w/tester) 58½″ x W 35½″ x L 58½″
Mid-Atlantic States, 1780-1800, Red stain, Hard Pine rails and head posts, White Pine headboard, Poplar foot posts

This bed is crowned by an arched tester supported by four turned posts. The head posts are simpler in design than the foot posts which are vase turned immediately above their juncture with the bed rails. At this same juncture, all four posts become square in section. Below the rails, the legs are turned. The rails and posts are secured by mortises and bed bolts. Two simple curves ornament the headboard.

Courtesy Henry Francis duPont Winterthur Museum

6. DOLL'S HIGH POST BED

H 34″ x W 14½″ x L 20″
England, c. 1800, Mahogany and Oak

Roofed with a pointed tester, this bed is supported by four posts. Nails from which valances were hung remain on the upper sides of the flat tester. The track for the bed curtains also survives. The oak head posts are rectangular in section and taper as they ascend from the floor. Each mahogany foot post rests on a ring turning and increases in size to a larger ring turning, above which each post becomes square in section at its juncture with the rails. Above the squared sections, ring turnings and a swirl reeded vase turning ornament each reeded and tapered post. At each post juncture, the oak bed rails flare downward in a typically English manner. This bed is held together by bed bolts – a rare occurrence in miniature beds. The headboard has an interesting cutout configuration of French curves.

Courtesy Greenfield Village and Henry Ford Museum

7. DOLL'S BED

H 17⅞″ x W 10½″ x L 14⅜″
Philadelphia, 1811, Mahogany

The tester of this Sheraton bed is lapped in the corners and pierced with iron nails that continue into the four posts. While the head and foot posts are similar in outline, above the level of the bed rails, four carved sections decorate each foot post. The upper and lower sections contain carved acanthus leaves; the two middle sections are boldly reeded vase shapes. The four sections are divided and further embellished by varying sizes of ring turnings. This carving is similar to that on the Ephraim Haines pieces made for Stephen Girard between 1806 and 1807. The posts are square in section at their juncture with the bed rails. The upper corners of the square sections are chamfered and end in lamb's-tongues. Below the juncture, the posts become circular and are ornamented by disc and ring turnings. As in the standard size beds of the period, the bed rails support a stretched piece of fabric laced to small pegs. This cloth supported the mattress. This bed, similar in quality to the best of the large beds of the period, was made for Miss Johnson of Upsala. Tradition has it that it was made when she was seven years old.

Courtesy Upsala Foundation

7

8. EARLY 19TH CENTURY DOLL'S HIGH POST BED AND BED FURNITURE

H 15″ x W 14″ x L 20″
c. 1800, Walnut and Pine

The following photographic essay describes each phase of the assembly and dressing of an early 19th century high post bed. The manner in which this miniature is dressed is the same manner in which a standard size bed would be dressed. In this particular bed hooks are attached to the bed rails. We have not seen hooks on full size beds, which used bed bolts instead.

35

No. 8A The bed unassembled.

No. 8B The bed assembled.

No. 8C The skirt partially tied.

No. 8D The full mattress and the addition of the bolster.

No. 8E The notched mattress and the manner in which the skirt is tied around the corners.

No. 8F The method of folding the bolster cover, sheet and blanket.

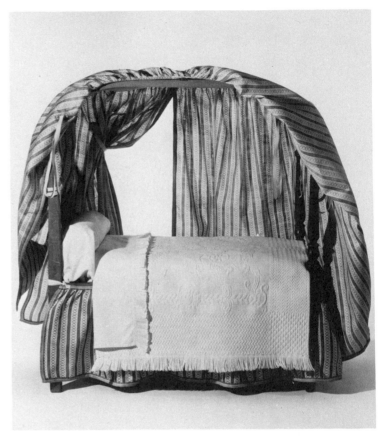

No. 8G The addition of the bed spread and bed curtains, hung up but pulled back to reveal the interior.

No. 8H The bed ready for use. Note how the curtains are tied back.

No. 8I The bed as it was used with the curtains closed.

Courtesy Greenfield Village and Henry Ford Museum

9. DOLL'S FOLDING HIGH POST BED

H 18¼" x W 10¾" x L 18"—L (folded) 5⅝"
Scotland, 1820, Mahogany, Brass finials

In order to conserve space, folding beds were used in the 18th century. Standard size English folding beds are built of mahogany and display a great sophistication of design. Most standard size American folding beds are made of painted maple and are rather unsophisticated. To conceal the bottom of the mattress when the bed was folded, curtains would have hung from the tester.

Courtesy Mrs. L. J. Torno, Jr.

10. CHILD'S LOW POST BED

H 19" x W 35⅝" x L 46⅛"
Possibly Pennsylvania, 1790-1850, Painted, Pine

This child's bed stands on four turned legs capped by large mushroom-like knobs. The bed rails are moulded at the top edge and are fastened to the posts with mortices and bed bolts. The slightly arched headboard has its upper corners cut away and circular notches formed on each end. The foot-board is straight edged.

Courtesy Henry Francis duPont Winterthur Museum

11A   11B

11. DOLL'S LOW POST BEDS

This collection of doll's low post beds is arranged to show a succession of styles. It is interesting to note that while almost no early standard size beds have footboards, most doll's low post beds do. Although doll's beds seldom have bed bolts, they otherwise conform to the standard size beds of the early 19th century.

No. 11A, a rope bed, has deeply cut out mushroom finials. Its round bed rails are an unusual feature found on standard size beds between Pittsburgh and Erie in western Pennsylvania.

Several beds demonstrate the different methods used for supporting the mattress. A canvas nailed to the bed rails of No. 11C acts as a mattress support, while No. 11B, with turnings similar to a Brewster chair, and No. 11H, a miniature Victorian spool bed, have slat supported mattresses. While No. 11D is a conventional rope bed, the mattress of No. 11E

11C

43

is supported by ropes around pegs.

Nos. 11F and 11G are similar in that they resemble the sleigh bed style. No. 11F suggests a sleigh bed in its curved headboard and footboard. No. 11F, an Empire bed, demonstrates that at this point in the development of style the side rails have become higher and thinner and have lost the square section used on earlier types.

11D

11E

11F

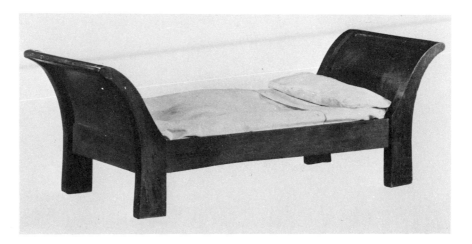

No. 11G is decorated with a Victorian type of applied moulding and feet similar to No. 128. Also in the Victorian style is No. 11I which has applied carving on the headboard. This bed is similar to many of the beds "Lincoln slept in."

Nos. 11F, 11G, 11H and 11I have flat side rails. This style originated in the Empire period and continues in today's production beds.

Courtesy Greenfield Village and Henry Ford Museum

11G

11H

11I

12. DOLLHOUSE BED STEPS

H 6″ x W 4¼″ x L 4¼″ (Step height 2″)
Voegler, Philadelphia, 1836, Mahogany

These American dollhouse bed steps are fantastically rare. The rails and back are rounded on top. The six decoratively turned legs taper to slim ankles above ball feet. The steps, surrounded by rectangular frames, are carpeted with a small piece of leather tacked down by ornamental tacks.

Courtesy Chester County Historical Society

13. MINIATURE DAYBED

H 9¾″ x W 5⅞″ x L 10¾″
England, Late 17th century, Beechwood

This William and Mary daybed has a crested cane back with carved scrolls supported by two half-round finial topped stiles which form the back legs. The frame is supported by two pairs of legs which are connected by turned side and cross stretchers. the disc turned stiles and legs stand on ball feet and are square in section at their junctures with the back slats, seat rails and stretchers. This piece is in superb original condition and shows great shrink and natural distress.

Courtesy Victoria and Albert Museum

14. DOLL'S COUCH

H 14¾" x W 14" x L 32"
Pennsylvania, 1840, Walnut; Pine (secondary)

This simple Empire couch is typical of the less
sophisticated and inexpensive furniture of this era.
(It is similar to example 282, *American Furniture,
The Federal Period, 1785–1825* by Charles Montgomery, but is without the refinement of outline or
detail of the Winterthur example.) The exposed
crest rail is refined with a moulded step and rounded
edges. The same moulding embellishes the seat rail.
The legs have simple scroll feet of pleasing proportion, but are without the refinement or embellishment found in No. 128. The couch is covered with
red velvet secured to the frame by brass headed tacks.

Courtesy William Penn Memorial Museum

BLANKET CHESTS

15. CHILD'S BLANKET CHEST

H 22½" x W 18½" x D 13¼"
Enfield, Connecticut, *c.* 1720, Pine

The top of this chest has a moulded edge and hinges on cotter key pins. For strength, under each end are fastened battens which, when the chest is closed, fit against the sides of the case. Although the chest appears to contain three drawers, the top two drawers are simulated and suggested by half-round moulding. The functional drawer is opened by two original wooden knobs. The lower end of the side continues to make a simple bracket foot. The most charming feature of this chest is the style of the heavily shod and boldly turned ball feet. (See *Connecticut Furniture of the 17th and 18th Century* by the Wadsworth Atheneum, illus. 53.)

Courtesy Mrs. Henry Clark

16. MINIATURE BLANKET CHEST

H 14½" x W 22½" x D 12⅞"
Windsor, Connecticut, 1720, Maple and Poplar

This chest has a boldly moulded top and is decorated with applied double-arched moulding to suggest a chest of drawers. Double-arched mouldings are usually found on the chest cases of drawers and highboys in the William and Mary style, and are generally used to outline the drawer openings. The base has a small quarter-round moulding and stands on vigorously turned ball feet. The red paint is original. (See *Connecticut Furniture of the Seventeenth and Eighteenth Century* by the Wadsworth Atheneum, exx. 73, 74, 75.)

Courtesy Wadsworth Atheneum

17. AMERICAN MINIATURE BLANKET CHEST

H 20½″ x W 22¾″ x D 12¾″
Robert Crossman, Taunton, Massachusetts, 1707-1799, Pine

This magnificent example of a painted miniature blanket chest has a moulded edge to the top, cotter key hinges, and applied half-round moulding decorating the case. The feet are made from continuations of the one board ends. The fanciful trees and strange birds are a variation from the usual and an inexpensive attempt to emulate European inlaid chests. This design, however, is less concise and more American than, for instance, example 103 in Nutting's *Furniture Treasury*. Except that it has two drawers instead of one, Nutting's Example 104 is a more closely related example.

Courtesy Art Institute of Chicago

18. MINIATURE BLANKET CHEST

H 10½″ x W 19¾″ x D 11″
Pennsylvania, *c.* 1720, Walnut, Chestnut inlay

Hinged on strong cotter key hinges, the top of this chest has a moulded edge with a large overhang, and is strengthened by large crude battens. The front corners of the case are dovetailed in a decorative manner. The elaborately scalloped lock is larger and placed lower than the locks on other American miniature chests we have seen. It may have been saved from the remains of an older destroyed European blanket chest. The front of the case is decorated with stylized stars and a small inlaid heart. The most unusual features are the fanciful shape of the feet and the intricately scalloped skirt. The size of the front feet and the suggestion of a center foot are features found on some large Pennsylvania chests. Inside the chest is a standard type till, at the back of which is an unusual smaller till.

Courtesy Herbert Schiffer Antiques

19. MINIATURE BLANKET CHEST

H 8″ x W 13¾″ x D 8½″
Pennsylvania (probably Chester County), *c.* 1729 or 1759,
Walnut; Poplar (Secondary)

Small handsome strap hinges join the case of this chest to the rectangular top in which the initials "P.B." are inlaid in putty. A complex moulding, applied to the front and sides of the top, is repeated at the base. Decorative dovetails embellish the front corners of the case. Also on the front of the case is a Chippendale escutcheon and putty inlay which forms the date 1759 or 1729. The chest stands on wide, fancifully cut bracket feet to which some restoration has been made.

Courtesy Mrs. Herbert F. Schiffer

20. MINIATURE DOWER CHEST

H 17″ x W 23″ x D 13″
Bermuda, 1740, Walnut; Cedar (secondary)

This miniature dower chest has a moulded top and distinctive dovetailed corners are utilized as a decorative feature. A very pronounced compound base moulding stands above a scalloped skirt. The chest is supported by cabriole legs which terminate in trifid feet. Standard size Bermuda chests are extremely rare, but this miniature chest may be unique. (See *Antiques Magazine,* January 1945.)

Courtesy Mrs. J. Austin duPont

21. MINIATURE BLANKET CHEST

H 7½" x W 15⅜" x D 8½"
Chester County, Pennsylvania, 1725-1775, Walnut

The rectangular top of this chest is surrounded on the front and sides by a step and thumbnail moulding. The case, embellished by exposed dovetails at its front corners, is decorated with Chester County line and berry inlay. It is interesting that the scribe marks can be clearly seen. These were made by the compass in order to swing the curves of the vines. This particular inlay is an exception in that it has leaves. The inlay is usually composed of holly and cherry, but sometimes the berries are of chestnut or poplar. (See Schiffer, *Furniture and Its Makers of Chester County, Pennsylvania,* exx. 121, 127, and 128.) The base moulding reflects that of the chest top. Turned ball feet which have been restored support the chest.

Courtesy Henry Francis duPont Winterthur Museum

22. MINIATURE DOWER CHEST

H 9½" x W 11⅜" x D 7¼"
Pennsylvania, 1760, Cherry and Walnut; Poplar (secondary)

A decorative moulding surrounds the top of this chest which retains its original strap hinges. Dovetails and an inlaid star, around which is a line of inlay, decorate the case front. The lips of the single drawer are moulded. Scalloped bracket feet support the moulded base.

Courtesy Mrs. Herbert F. Schiffer

23. MINIATURE BLANKET CHEST

H 10″ x W 14″ x D 7½″
Chester County, Pennsylvania, 1770, Walnut

This chest has an applied moulding at the edge of its top, in the center of which is an inlaid star surrounded by string inlay with concave corners. Dovetails on the front corners form a decorative device. Surrounded by a wide band with invected corners and pointed ends, a stylized parrot perched on a spray of clover leaves and tulips decorates the case. The parrot is the Carolina parakeet, now extinct, which was common to southeast Pennsylvania until the late 1840s. The clover leaves resemble three-berry inlays. (See Schiffer, *Furniture and Its Makers of Chester County, Pennsylvania,* p. 168.) The drawers are decorated by a line of string inlay with concave corners. The knobs may be original. Rather crude ball feet support the heavy base moulding. Despite this chest's ball feet, heavy moulding and early style decoration, the delicacy of the pointed dovetails suggests that it was made toward the end of the Chippendale period. The escutcheon is decorated with an inlaid heart. This piece retains its original simple butt hinges and has an unusual secret drawer in back of a false front.

Courtesy Mrs. Herbert F. Schiffer

DETAIL NO. 23

24. BLANKET CHEST

H 29⅜″ x W 52″ x D 23″
Chester County, Pennsylvania, *c.* 1770, Walnut: Poplar
(secondary)

This full scale chest, with the enclosed pattern of
bird and vines, is similar to No. 23. The feet on this
chest are not original.

Courtesy Mrs. Herbert F. Schiffer

25. MINIATURE BLANKET CHEST

H 10" x W 17½" x D 9¾"
Delaware Valley, 1750, Walnut, White Cedar (secondary)

The top of this chest is moulded and its single drawer is lipped. Exposed dovetails decorate the front corners and front feet. The case rests on a heavy cove moulding above bracket feet flanked by deeply ornamented scalloping. White cedar, from the swamps of New Jersey, is found in the drawer bottoms of Pennsylvania and New Jersey furniture.

Courtesy Mrs. Herbert F. Schiffer

26. MINIATURE BLANKET CHEST

H 7¾" x W 14⅞" x D 8½"
Chester County, Pennsylvania, 1773, Walnut

This chest has a boldly moulded top to which the
two side mouldings are applied. Around the edges,
the top is decorated by a line of putty which curves
inward at the corners. In the center is an elaborate
design reminiscent of the Daniel Merrill designs for
17th century gardens. "Johannes" is written above
the design, and "Mosser" below it. At the corners
of the design the date 1773 is incised. The chest is
ornamented with architectural details. Flat pilasters
separate three arched and sunken panels on the
upper front of the case. In each panel is a putty-filled
tulip flanked by two leaves and standing on a mound
of steps and curves. Below each panel is a drawer.
The chest stands on a boldly moulded base. Putty
inlay is also seen in No. 19. (See also Schiffer,
*Furniture and Its Makers of Chester County, Penn-
sylvania*, exx. 131, 132, and Stoudt, *Early Pennsylvania Arts and Crafts*, fig. 75, 83.)

Courtesy Henry Francis duPont Winterthur Museum

27. MINIATURE BLANKET CHEST

H 12½″ x W 19½″ x D 10½″
Lancaster County, Pennsylvania, 1770, Walnut; Pine and
Poplar (secondary)

This rare walnut chest has a moulded top and concealed dovetailing at the front corners. The front is
embellished with raised crisp carving of fanciful
wheat and shells. The two lipped drawers are ornamented with stylized, carved shells so large they
expand above the center of the drawer tops. This
carving is not applied, but is cut from the carcass.
The motif of wheat carving and stylized shells is
found on many of the pieces of furniture attributed
to the Bachman family. Inside the chest, which rests
on a heavy case moulding above deeply cut ogee feet,
is a partly moulded till.

Courtesy Mrs. J. Austin duPont

28. CHILD'S BLANKET CHEST

H 19″ x W 29½″ x D 15½″
Lancaster County, Pennsylvania, *c*. 1770, Cherry

The top edge of this chest is moulded; cock-beaded edges surround the three drawers with interior desk pulls. An intaglio carved sunflower in a crude basket adorns the front. Vines, tendrils and leaves which are carved from the carcass move in fanciful scrolls and curves above the sunflower. The corners are ornamented with quarter-columns decorated with carved vines and the ends have large pierced intaglio carved shells surrounded with gouge work. Perhaps this style of carving, often referred to as Bachman, ought to be called Lancaster County style. (See No. 27.) The cove moulded base rests on scrolled ogee feet.

Courtesy Mrs. J. Austin duPont

29. MINIATURE BLANKET CHEST

H 9⅛" x W 16¾" x D 10⅜"
Pennsylvania, 1785, Original paint, Poplar bottom, Pine sides

A step and thumbnail moulding edges the top front, the sides of which have applied mouldings as in Nos. 12 and 15. The lid bears a central circle with a banded and saw-toothed border enclosing a multicolored pinwheel. This circle is flanked by pear-shaped two-handled vases containing leafy tulip plants on which birds are perched. The design is in red, black, blue and yellow on a white background. Underneath the lid which is secured to the case by strap hinges is painted in red

FE. BER. Y
.1785.
.CA.SL.

These initials might signify the owner's intention of marriage.

Each half of the front panel bears a two-handled vase containing tulips, pinnate leaves and a large stylized blossom. Across the top is the date 1785. The colors are red, black and tan on a white background. (See Lichten, *Folk Art of Rural Pennsylvania,* p. 90.)

At either end, also in red, black and tan on white, is a male horseback rider flanked by tree-like flowering plants. (See Davidson, *The American Heritage History of Colonial Antiques,* ex. 521.)

The case rests on a moulding of which the bracket feet are extensions.

Courtesy Henry Francis duPont Winterthur Museum

30. DOLL'S BLANKET CHEST

W 7½" x W 12½" x D 6½"
Jonestown, Pennsylvania, *c.* 1775-1810, Original paint, Pine, Walnut feet

Applied moulded lips adorn the edge of the top of this chest, the case of which is supported on a simple base moulding above four ogee feet. Dovetails are visible at the corners of the case. The lid and front of the chest are decorated by yellow tombstone shaped panels bordered by red bands. In each panel is a vase containing leafy tulip forms in green, brown, red and yellow. The decorations are similar to those done by Christian Seltzer and John Rank in Jonestown at the end of the 18th century.

Courtesy Henry Francis duPont Winterthur Museum

30

31. MINIATURE BLANKET CHEST

H 9″ x W 15½″ x D 8¼″
Western Pennsylvania, c. 1800, Mahogany, Maple inlay

An inlaid urn, a motif popular during the Classical Period, decorates the moulded-edged lid of this blanket chest. Similar urns are seen on the escutcheons of furniture made by such cabinetmakers as John and Thomas Seymour. (See Montgomery, *American Furniture, The Federal Period, 1788–1825*, ex. 186.) In the front of the chest is a keyhole surrounded by a simple brass edge. The inlay decoration on the front consists of two doves perched above a basket on which are written the initials "M.H." A broad band of light inlay trims the base which stands on simple bracket feet.

Courtesy Mrs. J. Austin duPont

32. MINIATURE BLANKET CHEST

H 17″ x W 18½″ x D 10″
William Lloyde, Springfield, Mass., 1807, Mahogany and Satinwood; Pine (secondary)

A line of compound inlay adorns the front edge of this chest's top, and is repeated across the base. (See Montgomery, *American Furniture, The Federal Period, 1788–1825*, ex. 32.) A simulated drawer bordered by a line of light contrasting inlay is situated above a functional drawer. Light colored panels with inset quarter-circular corners surrounding a diamond shaped pattern decorate the drawers. Unusual contrasting pieces of banding above, below and at each end, also embellish each drawer. The skirt is fancifully scalloped and the case stands on delicate French feet. The maker's signature is written inside the case.

Courtesy Greenfield Village and Henry Ford Museum

DETAIL NO. 32

33. MINIATURE BLANKET CHEST

H 14½″ x W 23½″ x D 12¾″
Ohio, 1820, Cherry; Poplar and Walnut (secondary)

An applied moulding in the Empire style edges the top and base of his chest. The escutcheon is inlaid with light colored wood shaped like an elongated diamond. The facade is ornamented with two burled hearts flanking a light wood star. These are surrounded by two wide bands of burled walnut. The bracket feet and scalloping are extremely provincial Hepplewhite.

Courtesy Mr. and Mrs. Edward Stvan

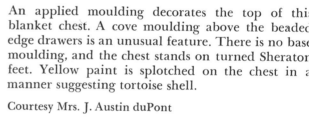

34. MINIATURE BLANKET CHEST

H 3¾″ x W 12″ x D 6¼″
Pennsylvania, c. 1830, Pine, yellow paint, smoke decoration

An applied moulding decorates the top of this blanket chest. A cove moulding above the beaded edge drawers is an unusual feature. There is no base moulding, and the chest stands on turned Sheraton feet. Yellow paint is splotched on the chest in a manner suggesting tortoise shell.

Courtesy Mrs. J. Austin duPont

35. MINIATURE BLANKET CHEST

H 9¾″ x W 13″ x D 6¾″
Ohio, 1830, Maple

The use of vigorously striped wood gives this chest its principle design. The edge of the top is applied. The case is plain except for exposed dovetails at the front corners and an inlaid escutcheon in the shape of an elongated diamond. A vigorous early moulding surrounds the base which rests on Sheraton turned feet.

Courtesy John Litten

36. MINIATURE BLANKET CHEST

H 5″ x W 9″ x D 5¼″
America, Mid-19th century, Mahogany, Bone feet and handles

A brass hasp secures the domed lid of this chest which stands on bone feet. The sides slant outward to give it more stability. At each end is a bone support intended to hold a braided rope handle. A spectacular inlaid eagle with a shield-shaped American flag on its chest decorates the lid. The eagle is set in an oval outlined by a lighter contrasting string inlay. Carved on the underside of the lid are the initials "C.E.M."

Courtesy Mrs. J. Austin duPont

DETAIL NO. 36

CHAIRS

37. CARVED MINIATURE ARMCHAIR

H 18½" x W 6½" x D 5¼" (Seat height 9")
England, *c.* 1690, Walnut

This chair which combines vigor of design with refinement of execution may be the finest surviving Stuart miniature chair in existence. Its surface shows the original chisel marks and still retains its old finish of Spanish brown stain. An elongated oval panel, filled with caning, forms the chair back. The upper peak of the oval is formed by the moulded pierced arch of the crest rail. This arch contains a carved and pierced cipher and is flanked by carved scrolls. An arch at the center of the bottom splat forms the lower part of the oval and balances the curve of the crest rail. (See Edwards, *The Shorter Dictionary of English Furniture*, fig. 38.) The crest rail is echoed in the front stretcher which contains an arch with a pierced design. (See Edwards, fig. 39.) The turned stiles (see Edwards, fig. 35) are decorated by fluted cylinders and form the back legs which flare backward at a 45 degree angle. This gives the chair its vigorous stance. The ram's horn knuckles of the moulded arms are one of the salient features of this chair. The arm supports and front legs are similarly trumpet turned and terminate in trumpet turned feet. (See Edwards, fig. 48.) The moulded seat rails form a frame for the cane seat.

Courtesy Mrs. Herbert F. Schiffer

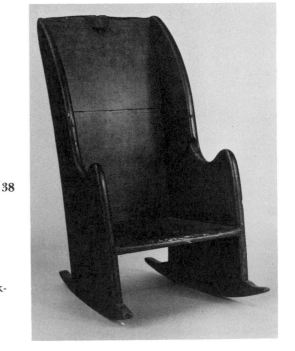

38

38. MINATURE ROCKING CHAIR

H 21⅛" x W 11" (Seat height 5½")
New England, 18th century, Pine, Poplar

Although a far cruder version, this miniature rocking chair is similar in construction to No. 39.

Courtesy Yale University Art Gallery
Mabel Brady Garvan Collection

39

40. MINIATURE ARMCHAIR

H 8¾″ x W 4¾″ (Seat height 3″)
New England, c. 1700-1750, Maple

Vase and ball finials top this chair's stiles which are decorated with ring turnings. The crest rail is turned and divided by sausage-link and disc swellings, a design which is echoed in the lower rail of the back. The turned spindle balusters are ornamented with elongated vase and disc turnings; this design is enlarged and repeated in the box stretchers. The cylindrical arm supports are crowned with turnings suggesting the mushroom turned arms of Pilgrim furniture. (See Nutting, *Furniture of the Pilgrim Century,* exx. 304, 305, 315.) The front legs which terminate in blunt arrow feet are decorated alternately by cylinders, and vase and disc turnings. This chair, including its rush seat, is entirely original and has a fine patina. This chair is later than the New England Carver chairs suggested by its upper half; the lower half and arm supports conform to the best of New Jersey and Pennsylvania slat-back chairs, a fact which indicates its possible later date. (See Nutting, ex. 421.) This miniature chair was purchased from the descendants of an early Dutch family, NAUGLE or NAGLE as listed in Bailey's *Genealogical Index of Pre-Revolutionary Dutch Houses and Families.* The Naugle chair has features in common with groups of slat-back chairs found in northern New Jersey and southern New York. The ring turnings, finials, finish and termination of the front and back legs suggest Hudson River Valley or Hackensack River Valley origin.

Courtesy Mr. and Mrs. Ray Blake

39. CHILD'S POTTY ROCKER

H 31″ x W 14″ x D 23½″ (Rocker length)
America, 18th century, Walnut

Put together with wooden pegs, this chair is made of six boards—the back, two sides, two rockers and seat. The seat which has a utilitarian hole holds the other parts together. The outline of the sides suggests medieval church furniture. Such refinements as the cutout heart, the shape of the sides, the moulding at the front edge of the seat and the elaborate rockers make this chair the best of its type. (See Stoudt, *Early Pennsylvania Arts and Crafts,* fig. 74.)

Courtesy Philadelphia Museum of Art

40

41. CHILD'S PILGRIM MUSHROOM ARMCHAIR

H 25¼″ x W 15¼″ x D 10¾″ (Seat height 6¾″)
New England, *c.* 1700, Red Maple

Mushroom armchairs are exceedingly rare, but children's examples are almost nonexistent. This chair is very successful in its design. The finials, consisting of two ring turnings topped by a slender-necked ball, rise well above the top splat. The stiles are cylindrical, interrupted by a ring turning between each splat. The arms, simple spindles, pierce the arm supports which are cylindrically turned and capped with applied mushroom discs. Four box stretchers strengthen the chair legs. The sides and back are simple spindles, but the front stretcher has three sausage turnings at its center. This chair retains its original black paint. (See Nutting, *Furniture of the Pilgrim Century,* ex. 369.)

Courtesy Wadsworth Atheneum

42. CHILD'S CORNER OR ROUND-A-BOUT CHAIR

H 20½″ x W 19½″ x D 19¼″
America, *c.* 1720, Hickory and Maple

This rare type child's chair is supported by three tall stiles crowned by unusual finials suggestive of saltshakers. This saltshaker motif is repeated as a turning in the front leg. With the exception of a bulbous turning just above the seat, each post is cylindrical to the floor. Two splats connect the stiles; one splat is damaged, but the other bears an interesting scalloped top. Simple leather-covered box stretchers form the seat, and two sets of box stretchers strengthen the legs.

Courtesy Art Institute of Chicago

43. CHILD'S SLAT-BACK ARMCHAIR

H 27½" x W 13¾" x D 10½" (Seat height 7")
New England, c. 1720, Red Maple

The most prominent feature of this simple rush-seated chair is its finials which tower over the top slat. The chair's three slats curve upward at the top center, but are straight-bottomed. Note that the top slat has lost some of its center curve. Both the back and front legs taper toward the top and have no ornamentation. More than an inch has been restored to all the feet. The arm spindles are turned just before they enter the supports. The box stretchers give evidence of having been whittled rather than turned. (See Nutting, *Furniture of the Pilgrim Century*, ex. 458.)

Courtesy Wadsworth Atheneum

44. CHILD'S SLAT-BACK ARMCHAIR

H 22½" x W 6¾" x D 11"
Pennsylvania, c. 1730, Traces of blue, white and red paint

Turned finials decorate this chair's back posts which are connected by three slats. For the child's comfort, the slats curve gracefully backward and upward. The slightly curved arms are notched in front of the arm supports and stiles. Vase turnings ornament the arm supports. Just below each arm is a cylindrical section pierced by a hole through which a rod is placed in order to keep the child in the chair. The box stretchers are simple spindles. This chair which was once painted shows its scribe marks. These are small guide lines which enable the joiner to see where to drill the holes for joining the stretchers, arms and slats.

Courtesy Wadsworth Atheneum

45. MINIATURE CANED ARMCHAIR

H 14½″ x W 8¼″ x D 5″
England or America, c. 1700, Walnut

This miniature armchair of superb quality is an extreme rarity. The convex sides of the crest rail ascend to a flat top. The scratch beaded stiles and crest rail enclose a caned back. The arms curve inward and then flare outward to terminate in thick deeply carved ram's horn knuckles. A cane seat is enclosed by vigorously curved and scalloped seat rails. Deeply curved turnings ornament the arm supports and are repeated on the H stretcher. The front legs have primitive cabriole knees and terminate in rudimentary Spanish feet. The back legs, connected by a double ball and disc stretcher, flare back boldly to give the chair a regal stance. (For a similar chair in a standard size see Horner, *Philadelphia Furniture 1682–1807*, ex. 15.)

Courtesy Mr. and Mrs. Theodore Kapnek

46. MINIATURE QUEEN ANNE ARMCHAIR

H 14½″ x W 6″ x D 8¼″
Hudson River Valley, c. 1720, Ash, Black paint

The style of this transitional miniature armchair lies between the William and Mary and the Queen Anne styles. Its crest rail is of the oxbow type found on so many New York and New Jersey chairs of Holland-Dutch influence. (See Downs, *American Furniture, Queen Anne and Chippendale Periods*, ex. 24.) The crest rail is supported by two turned stiles which form the cylindrical back legs, and by a simple Queen Anne splat. Each arm curves gently downward and then upward to terminate in a rudimentary knuckle which is similar to those found on No. 44. The arm supports continue as the front legs. They are alternately disc turned and circular in section and terminate in simple ball feet. The front stretcher has a double ball and disc turning; the side and back stretchers are simple spindles. The chair which has a rush seat retains its original black paint.

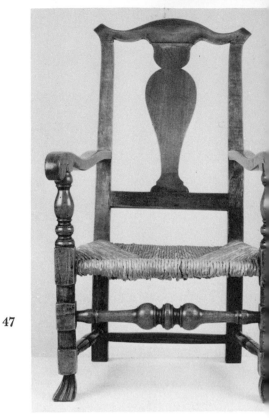

47. CHILD'S QUEEN ANNE ARMCHAIR

H 28″ x W 16″ x D 16¼″
New England, c. 1750, Maple and Ash

A serpentine crest rail, flanked by ears which curve backward, is a feature of this rare, rush-seated armchair which retains traces of its original paint. The back legs which are raked backward are rectangular in section and taper gracefully as they rise to meet the crest rail. The arms terminate in uncarved scrolls and are supported by baluster turned extensions of the front legs which stand on finely carved Spanish feet. While the side and back stretchers are rather simple, the front stretcher is very elaborate. Its arrow shaped ends flank a bold double ball and disc turning in the center.

Courtesy Henry Francis duPont Winterthur Museum

46

48. MINIATURE QUEEN ANNE SIDE CHAIR

H 13¼" x W 5½" x D 5½" (Seat height 6")
Ireland, *c.* 1720, Mahogany

Very closely grained heavy mahogany, probably of Cuban origin, was used in this Irish miniature arm-chair. The crest rail curves up to the center and is outlined by a bead that descends to two carved volutes which curve inward. The stiles are S shaped and, to a certain extent, conform to the shape of the solid splat. The moulded seat rail surrounds a rectangular slip seat which was carved from one piece of wood and shows signs of having been upholstered many times. Whereas the back legs are round in section below the seat rail and flare backward to terminate square in section in a manner similar to that found on some New York chairs, the front legs have cabriole knees with deep glue blocks carved in cyma curves which end in crisply carved volutes. The legs descend to a very fine ankle and terminate in rather crudely shaped trifid feet. (See Edwards, *The Shorter Dictionary of English Furniture,* exx. 34, 62.)

Courtesy Mr. and Mrs. Theodore Kapnek

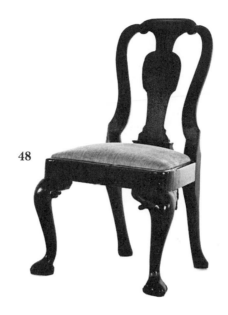

48

49. MINIATURE QUEEN ANNE SIDE CHAIR

H 27" x W 13¾" x D 12"
England, *c.* 1740, Mahogany

This mahogany miniature Queen Anne side chair has a yoked crest rail similar to ex. 138, *American Furniture of the Museum of Fine Arts, Boston* by Richard Randall, Jr., and stiles similar to ex. 137 in the same book. The solid splat is flanked by stiles that are round in section until they join the seat rails, at which point they become square. Below the seat rail the stiles form the back legs; they are round in section and flare strongly backward. The seat rail contains a slip seat, is scalloped in front and has a most unusual side profile. The cabriole legs are flanked by glue blocks and descend to thin ankles which terminate in very flat pad feet.

Courtesy Mr. and Mrs. Theodore Kapnek

50. CHILD'S QUEEN ANNE ARMCHAIR

H 30½" x W 17¼" x D 13¾" (Seat height 12¼")
England, *c.* 1730, Walnut, Veneer over Beech

This chair would make a beautifully proportioned full size chair. The crest rail is ornamented with a deeply dished yoke. The solid splat conforms to the shape of the stiles which curve sharply inward and then gently outward. The S shaped arms are hollowed out toward the back of the arm rests, become round in section toward the front, and then curve outward in a carved scroll at the handrest. The arm supports curve backward and are attached to the outside of the balloon shaped vertical walnut veneer seat rail which contains a slip seat. Simple glue blocks and carved shells above pendant husks ornament the cabriole legs which descend to a graceful ankle and slipper foot. Flanking the shells are carved cyma curves which end in volutes at the top and bottom. The back legs are square in section at their juncture with the seat rail and become round in section as they descend to join the side stretchers. At this point they become square and continue, flaring backward vigorously, to the floor.

Courtesy Colonial Williamsburg

51. CHILD'S QUEEN ANNE ARMCHAIR

H 26¼" x W 17¾" x D 13½" (Seat height 11")
England, *c.* 1720, Mahogany

An interesting feature of this chair is the unusual shape of its splat which joins the stiles opposite their juncture with the arms. (See Edwards, *The Shorter Dictionary of English Furniture,* ex. 80.) The arms which are rectangular in section terminate in carved ram's horn knuckles. The arm supports curve sharply backward and are attached to the outside of the balloon seat frame containing a slip seat. The edge of the seat rail is moulded and its front surface is veneered. Echoing the shell carved into the crest rail, a carved shell on each cabriole knee rises to the edge of the seat rail. Each knee is flanked by volutes and glue blocks. (Note that the carving on this chair and on the two following armchairs is heavier and coarser than that on No. 50.) The front legs descend through a heavy ankle to a slipper foot and the back legs rake outward and flare into a modified Queen Anne pad foot. Under the seat rail is stamped in capital initials "I.D." It is not known if these are the mark of the owner or of the maker.

Courtesy Herbert Schiffer Antiques

52. CHILD'S QUEEN ANNE ARMCHAIR

H 27″ x W 18″ x D 12¾″ (Seat height 11½″)
England, *c.* 1740, Mahogany Veneer on Birch

Above pendant husks, a raised carved shell flanked by volutes embellishes the round crest rail of this armchair. The stiles curve to conform to the splat. The arms are flattened at their juncture with the stiles, but become round in cross-sections as they extend forward to become shepherd's crooks attached to the outside of the seat frame. Flame stitch covers the balloon shaped slip seat. The back legs are square in section where they join the seat rail, underneath which they flare slightly backward and terminate in simple pad feet. The cabriole front legs which terminate in claw and ball feet have raised carved shells above pendant husks flanked by carved cyma curves on the knees and seat rail. Numbered inside the seat rail, this chair may have been part of a set.

Courtesy Mr. and Mrs. Theodore Kapnek

53. CHILD'S ARMCHAIR

H 28″ x W 16″ x D 15″
England, *c.* 1740, Cuban or Indian Mahogany

This chair has an upholstered back and is partially upholstered over the seat rail. The beautifully dished arms taper and become round in section to form shepherd's crooks which are fastened to the outside of the seat rail. (See Edwards, *The Shorter Dictionary of English Furniture,* ex. 99.) In the center of the front seat rail is a carved inverted shell topped by a husk. (See Edwards, ex. 79.) With the addition of cyma curves and volutes, this shell motif is repeated on the cabriole front legs which terminate in crisply carved claw and ball feet. The cabriole back legs rake backward and terminate in rudimentary Spanish feet. (See Edwards, ex. 72.)

Courtesy Mrs. J. Austin duPont

54. CHILD'S TRANSITIONAL SIDE CHAIR

H 29" x W 17¾" x D 15⅞"
Philadelphia, c. 1760, Mahogany

This magnificently executed and very unusual transitional chair (Queen Anne to Chippendale) is tremendously rare. The double-S curved crest rail is flanked by crisply carved ears and in its center has a raised carved shell. The stiles are fluted and the unusual splat is solid. In the center of the seat rail is a raised, carved and inverted shell that extends below the lower edge. The cabriole front legs, flanked by plain glue blocks and decorated on the knees with crisply carved shells, terminate in claw and ball feet. The back stump legs are rectangular in section, deeply chamfered on all four corners and raked vigorously backward and toward the center. This chair has been handed down within the family of Thomas Commoroe Trotter (1823–1901), possibly a nephew of Joseph Trotter and grandnephew of Benjamin Trotter. It is surmised that this chair was made for Joseph Trotter II by his grandfather Joseph Trotter.

Courtesy Henry Francis duPont Winterthur Museum

55. MINIATURE CHIPPENDALE SIDE CHAIR

H 14" x W 8¾" x D 6¼"
America or England, c. 1750, Mahogany

The elaborate crest rail of this chair is outlined with a raised carved bead in reversing curves and its center is pierced by an asymmetrical heart, also outlined with a raised lip. The delicately pierced splat contains six carved volutes and is vigorously carved where the patterns cross. A raised carved bead outlines the inner and outer edges of the stiles. The gracefully curved rectangular seat rail has a moulded edge and contains a slip seat. The cabriole front legs, flanked by uncarved glue blocks, descend through fine ankles and terminate in crisply carved claw and ball feet. Unless it is intended to be a miniature slipper chair, this piece could legitimately be criticized for its proportions. The back appears to be too high in relation to the height of the seat.

Courtesy Mrs. J. Austin duPont

56. CHILD'S CHIPPENDALE SIDE CHAIR

H 28½″ x W 15″ x D 13″ (Seat height 12″)
America or England, c. 1760, Walnut

This provincial but pleasing side chair has a rich mellow patination. Its most distinctive characteristic is its crest rail which has deeply carved ears that rise and curve backward. The center of the crest rail is surmounted by a yoke with carved volutes. The fully pierced splat is slightly coarse but, nevertheless, is in balance with the vigor of the chair. The stiles widen as they descend to join the seat rail; from the seat rail to the floor, the stiles curve backward and are square in section. The slip seat is surrounded by a seat rail with a moulded top edge. The box stretchers are rectangular in section. A deeply cut bead embellishes the outside front corners of the two square front legs.

Courtesy Mrs. J. Austin duPont

57. CHILD'S SIDE CHAIR

H 30¼″ x W 15″ x D 13″ (Seat height 11½″)
Thomas Goddard, Newport, Rhode Island, Late 18th century, Walnut, Original finish

This child's side chair is of the type known as the ribbon or pretzel back chair. The stiles, connected by three pierced serpentine splats, are flat in front, round in back, and become square as they join the seat rail. (For similar splats see Montgomery, *American Furniture of the Federal Period*, ex. 81.) The back legs which are connected by a stretcher curve backward as they descend to the floor. The seat frame contains a rectangular rush seat and rests on tapered front legs. The front and back legs are connected by stretchers.

Courtesy John Walton, Inc.

58. DOLL'S SIDE CHAIR

H 6¾″ x W 3¾″ x D 3½″ (Seat height 3¾″)
Stover and Taylor, New York, c. 1790, Mahogany

The crest rail of this Hepplewhite chair is enhanced by a raised carved block at its center. (See Montgomery, *American Furniture, The Federal Period 1788–1825*, ex. 24.) The moulded stiles and crest rails enclose four moulded, reeded, carved and turned balusters. (See Montgomery, exx. 61, 62.) The heavy seat is bowed in front and covered with leather ornamented by swags of exposed brass tack heads. The bold, rectangular, tapered back legs which curve backward are continuations of the stiles. The reeded front legs taper through delicate ankles to spade feet. (See Montgomery, ex. 82.) One front leg has been repaired.

Courtesy Mrs. J. Austin duPont

59. MINIATURE ARMCHAIR

H 15¾" x W 10" x D 9" (Seat height 8")
Anne Arundel, Maryland, c. 1815, Ebony

The rectangular crest rail of this Sheraton armchair curves to conform to the sitter's back. The crest rail and the splat below it are embellished with carved lines outlining panels, a decorative device of the English Regency found on fine American Empire examples. The tops of the stiles rise above the crest rail, curl backward and are ornamented with applied turned bosses. The turned arms descend in graceful curves from their juncture with the top splat. Below the seat rail which contains a caned seat, the front legs, ornamented with ring turnings, taper to round feet. The square back legs taper slightly as they curve backward. (See Montgomery, *American Furniture, The Federal Period, 1788–1825*, ex. 70; Miller, *American Antique Furniture, A Book for Amateurs*, ex. 293; and Randall, *American Furniture in the Museum of Fine Arts,* ex. 182.)

Courtesy David Stockwell, Inc.

60. CHILD'S TUB CHAIR

H 21½" x W 14" x D 13"
George Bright, Boston, Massachusetts, c. 1800, Mahogany

Full scale tub chairs are uncommon, but a child's size chair such as this is extremely rare. This particular chair has great refinement. The exposed crest rail continues into the arms which are supported by freestanding reeded columns that continue downward to form the front legs. These arm supports become square in section at their juncture with the exposed seat rail. The reeded front legs taper to round spade feet; the square back legs taper and flare backwards. The leather upholstery is embellished with raised tack head decoration and the seat lifts to reveal that this is a potty chair. George Bright made similar chairs without reeding for the Boston State House. (See Montgomery, *American Furniture, The Federal Period, 1788–1825,* ex. 134.)

Courtesy David Stockwell, Inc.

61. CHILD'S ARMCHAIR

H 25" x W 13½" (Seat height 13")
Duncan Phyfe, New York, c. 1800, Mahogany

The curving crest rail of this chair has a raised border with a scratch beaded inner edge. Within this border is a sunken panel containing a typical raised carved Duncan Phyfe motif, wheat tied by a bow knot. (See Montgomery, *American Furniture, The Federal Period, 1788-1825,* exx. 66, 67, 68.) Immediately below the crest rail and above the reeded lower splat, is a crisply carved lyre, another device frequently found on American Empire furniture, and particularly on pieces made by Duncan Phyfe in New York. (See Montgomery, exx. 72A, 73.) Both the stiles and arms are reeded. Round turned bosses are applied on the outside edges of the junctions of the arm, crest rail, legs and seat rail. Above the reeded seat rail is a slip seat. The front legs have typical dog paw feet. (See Montgomery, ex. 74.) The rectangular tapered back legs curve slightly backward. This is a carefully executed piece with great refinement of detail and proportion.

Courtesy Mr. and Mrs. Robert Lee Gill

62. CHILD'S ARMCHAIR

H 18½" x W 13¼" x D 14¼"
New York, *c.* 1800-1820, Mahogany, Mahogany Veneer,
Oak frame, Pine seat rail

A raised panel of crotch veneer outlined by a deeply cut trench embellishes the back curving crest rail and lower splat of this chair. At each end is a raised and applied ornament. The arms which curve downward are moulded on their tops and front edges. The arm supports reverse and continue forward as the legs. The legs are moulded on the front edges as are the stiles which curve forward to form the two side seat rails. The seat lifts out. The back legs curve slightly backward. There is a chip in the right front leg. A high quality, beautifully designed and finished piece, this chair has many small refinements that are difficult to describe.

Courtesy Boston Museum of Fine Arts

63. DOLL'S CHAIRS

H 6¾" x W 3¾" x D 3¾" (Seat height 3¼")
Voegler, Philadelphia, *c.* 1836, Mahogany

These chairs are part of a set of two armchairs and four side chairs from a dollhouse made for the Darlington family in 1836. The flat crest rails, decorated by carved florets, are accentuated by delicately carved ears. The top edge of the curved center splat is scalloped. The back legs are extensions of the flat stiles, and the front legs are of the saber type. The seats lift out. (See Miller, *American Antique Furniture, A Book for Amateurs,* ex. 352.)

Courtesy Chester County Historical Society

65. MINIATURE FANCY SHERATON SIDE CHAIR

H 11" x W 7½" x D 6½"
New England, *c.* 1840, Maple, Original paint and designs

The stiles extend above the decorated crest rail of this miniature Sheraton chair. (See Lee, *The Ornamental Chair,* exx. 30, 62.) The center splat consists of four square bars divided by three rows of three balls per opening. This is a much more sophisticated splat than that on No. 64. Below the flat seat rail which is bent around a rush seat, (See Lee, ex. 45), the stiles descend to the floor as simple cylinders. (See Lee, ex. 62.) The front legs are decorated by ring turnings, but are far less sophisticated than previous examples. The side and back stretchers are simple spindles, while the front stretcher has three ring turnings. (See Nos. 69 and 81 in this book.)

64

64. CHILD'S FANCY SHERATON SIDE CHAIR

H 19¾" x W 13¾" x D 11¼"
New England, *c.* 1810, Original paint

Connecting the flat stiles which become the round back legs of this chair, are three very different splats. The first is the crest rail, flat and large enough to decorate; the center splat is curved backward and comprised of two square rails connected by three turned balls; and the third is solid like the crest rail, but narrower and striped across its center. The flat seat rail is bent around the balloon shaped rush seat. The tapered front legs are decorated with ring turnings and stripes of paint. The side and back stretchers are simple turned spindles, but the design of the center back splat is repeated with a slight difference in the front stretcher. Whereas the splat curves backward to conform to the sitter's back, the stretcher curves forward to conform to the seat above it. (For similar chairs, see Lee, *The Ornamented Chair,* and Montgomery, *American Furniture, The Federal Period, 1788–1825,* exx. 71, 469.)

66. MINIATURE FANCY SHERATON SIDE CHAIR

H 8½" x W 4¾" x D 4¼" (Seat height 4½")
Hitchcock, Alford and Co., Hitchcock, Conn., Maple or Birch, Original paint and decoration

The flat crest rail of this chair is curved to conform to the sitter's back. The stiles which are flat in front for ease of decoration become round as they approach their juncture with the seat rail, and taper as they continue to the floor. Flat side rails and a cylindrical front seat rail enclose the rush seat. The legs are connected by a stretcher in the back and by two simple turned spindles on each side. The front stretcher is missing. The front legs, decorated with sophisticated ball and ring turnings, begin to taper below the bottom stretcher and terminate in ball feet. (For similar legs see Lee, *The Ornamented Chair*, ex. 45.)

67. MINIATURE DENTIST CHAIR

H 12¼" x W 6⅝" x D (w/footrest) 12½"
Dr. Ira Allen Salmon, America, 1868-1877, Wood, Brass

A concave, padded and shaped headrest is attached to the top of this dentist's chair which is upholstered in green silk and has a high pointed back surrounded by a wooden moulding. The exposed crest rail descends into carved arms which represent swans' heads and necks. The serpentine front skirt has an applied panel and raised mouldings on the edges. The entire chair rests on a pedestal which supports an adjustable foot rest; this pedestal is supported by four brass cabriole legs. This chair, probably used as a teaching aid, was made by Dr. Ira Allen Salmon, dentist and lecturer at Harvard.

Courtesy Henry Francis duPont Winterthur Museum

68. CHILD'S VICTORIAN CHAIR

H 31⅝" x W 15" x D 15"
Belter, New York, *c.* 1860, Laminated rosewood

The crest rail of this child's chair is a continuation of the stiles which contain a splat of great complexity. The splat, a Victorian revival of carved Renaissance motifs, is curved and formed to the back of the seat rail. The seat frame is partially exposed. The cabriole front legs are unusual in that each has a carved floret immediately above its juncture with the seat rail. The round back legs curve backward and outward.

Courtesy Metropolitan Museum of Art

69. MINIATURE PAINTED PLANK SEAT CHAIR

H 14¼″ x W 7″ x D 7¾″ (Seat height 7″)
Wheeling, West Virginia, *c.* 1875, Poplar seat, Maple legs, Painted

This chair has an arched rectangular crest rail supported by two turned stiles. Each of the stiles and the three spindles they flank are decorated by a turned disc halfway between the crest rail and the plank seat. A larger version of the same type of turning is repeated on the two turned front legs. The turned back legs taper below the stretchers and flare back with notable rake. The legs are connected by four simply turned spindle box stretchers. The front stretcher has a decoration at its center similar to those on the stiles. This very late chair may have been a cabinetmaker's sample, of which very few existed. It was part of a group of chairs from a fitted suitcase. During the 1870s the country was covered extensively by salesmen for all types of products, and this group may have been salesmen's samples.

Courtesy H. C. Foster

70. CHILD'S WINDSOR ARMCHAIR

H (approx.) 12″
America, *c.* 1870

This very small captain's or fireman's chair is a Victorian machine version of the earlier Windsor chair. Captain's chairs of standard size are extremely comfortable. The curved crest rail is hollowed out in back and applied to the top of the continuous arm which curves out at each end. This arm is supported by seven spindles which are narrow at the top and bottom, but widen to a ring turning in the center. The slightly shaped plank has little chamfering. The legs have an excellent rake and stance and are decorated with ring and weak vase turnings. The H stretcher, with a greatly enlarged center, is more suggestive of an early Windsor chair.

Courtesy Mr. and Mrs. Theodore Kapnek

BED NO. 11

CHAIR NO. 37

BED NO. 11 B

HIGH CHAIR NO. 78   HOOP-BACK NO. 88   ARMCHAIR NO. 87

84

71. CHILD'S SHAKER ROCKING CHAIR

H 25¾" x W 16¼" x D 19" (Seat height 12")
Shaker Community, Mount Lebanon, New York, c. 1875-1900

In design this child's chair is a combination of a Pilgrim armchair and a simple factory product. (See No. 41.) Each of the three splats is straight bottomed and slightly arched at its top edge. The back stiles which are crested with simple finials widen as they descend and terminate in deep rectangular rockers. The curved arms are slightly spread and are ornamented at their top front edges with an applied mushroom. The seat is a simple frame covered by the woven bright blue and white tape often found on Shaker furniture. The arm supports have a slight ornamental turning, but from the seat down the legs are cylindrically turned. The box stretchers are simple turned dowels. All parts of the design feature an economy of line and an eye to profitable factory production. The chair bears a strong resemblance to modern Danish furniture, much of which has been influenced by early Shaker design. The chair is marked with a stencil on the back of the bottom splat, "Shakers Trade Mark NO 1/Mount Lebanon, New York". This chair shows the difference in ideas of American design of the same period. Compare this chair to No. 68 made at approximately the same time. One back post has been repaired and the seat has been replaced. The replacement of the seat is considered of trivial importance if it is replaced in an appropriate manner. (See Andrews and Andrews, *Shaker Furniture,* Plate 15.)

Courtesy New Hampshire Historical Society

72. CHILD'S SHERATON STYLE PLANK SEAT CHAIR

H 17¼" x W 12¾" x D 9½"
Lancaster County, Pennsylvania, c. 1880, Brown, gold stenciling

This is a Pennsylvania Dutch version of a fancy or painted Sheraton chair of 1810. The rectangular crest rail, large enough to decorate, is supported by two turned stiles which have a painted ball turning, and by two splats which are shaped for painting. The plank seat is simple in outline and has no chamfering and little shape. The two front legs have ball and vase turnings. All four legs have a great deal of rake which gives the chair a bold stance. The importance of this chair lies in its decoration by G. Lane or some contemporary artist. G. Lane decorated chairs, boxes, buckets, cups and other small pieces of wood at the Lane Brother factory in Lititz after 1870 and up to the early 20th century. (See Stoudt, *Early Pennsylvania Arts and Crafts.*)

Courtesy Philip Hammerslaugh

73

73. CHILD'S HIGHCHAIR

H 36″ x W 16″ x D 12¾″
New England, *c.* 1660-1690, Ash

Deeply cut, crisply turned finials rise above the cresting of this brewster type highchair. Three parallel horizontal spindles connect the two stiles and below them there are three turned vertical spindles. The arms are turned spindles which pierce the arm supports. Under each arm are three vertical spindles similar to but shorter than the three vertical spindles in the back. The arm supports continue as simple cylinders. Below the seat the front legs are pierced with rectangular chamfered battens used to support a simple footrest. The four legs are strengthened by the very simplest of turned spindle box stretchers.

Courtesy Art Institute of Chicago

74. CHILD'S HIGHCHAIR

H 21¼″ x W 15¾″ x D 12¼″
England, 1687, Oak

A finial crowns the large square section of this wainscot highchair; the other finial is missing. On their inside edges, the stiles have double-arch beading reminiscent of the double-arch mouldings found surrounding the drawers on William and Mary furniture. (See No. 100.) A considerably worn, highly arched crest rail on which is carved the date 1687 is one of the more important features of this piece. The bottom of the crest rail is decorated with reeding done by the same plane that reeded the stiles. The crest rail and the stiles enclose a flat sunken panel. The arms are a cruder version of the standard size chair shown in Edwards, *The Shorter Dictionary of English Furniture,* ex. 17. The same type of arm is used on American wainscot chairs. The arm supports are decorated with vigorous vase turnings. Notched inward to receive the legs, the plank seat has a small amount of overhang. The skirt is simple and the arm supports and back stiles continue in rectangular section to form the legs which are greatly raked, but lack between 10″ and 15″ of their original length. The fact that this is a dated wainscot chair forces one to disregard such faults.

Courtesy Victoria and Albert Museum

74

75. CHILD'S HIGHCHAIR

H 38" x W13½" (Seat height 18")
Milford, Conn., Mid-18th century, Maple, Painted black

The back posts of this chair are topped by finials of an unusual Connecticut design. The crest rail has a scalloped outside line pierced in the center by a heart, a decoration found in the cresting of many Connecticut chairs. This chair, related to a group of chairs called heart and crown chairs, appears in *Connecticut Furniture of the Seventeenth and Eighteenth Centuries* by the Wadsworth Atheneum. (See exx. 206-212, 213, 220, 221, 222, 224, and 234 in the same publication.) The stiles are decorated by ornamental turnings from the crest rail to the seat, below which they are cylindrical in shape. The back consists of three vertical, moulded, flat balusters between the crest rail and a horizontal splat. The shaped arms are deeply notched behind the arm rests and below the arms is another turned member connecting the back stiles with the arm supports. Each cylindrically turned leg is interrupted by two turnings which resemble ball feet. To give the chair more stability, there is some rake to the legs. This rush seated chair is thought to have been given to Elizabeth Davidson of Milford, Connecticut by her father.

Courtesy Connecticut Historical Society

76

76. CHILD'S HIGHCHAIR

H 34½" x W 17⅞" x D 19"
America, 18th century, Maple and Ash, Painted black

Simple finials ornament the undecorated stiles of this slat-back highchair. The two slats are shaped and arched in the center. The arm supports are vase turned, as are the front and back legs except where they join the seat rail and the two sets of box stretchers. At these points the legs become cylindrical. The legs terminate in two rather crude turnings, the top suggesting a ball, and the bottom a cylinder. The seat is covered with splinting and the chair is painted black.

Courtesy Yale University Art Gallery
Mabel Brady Garvan Collection

77. CHILD'S HIGHCHAIR

Chair: H 15½" x W (back) 11½" x W (front) 13⅜"
Table: H 11" x W 14⅜"
England, c. 1800, Mahogany

77

By unscrewing the wing nut that connects the center stretcher of this chair to the top of the table, this type of highchair can be separated from its base to form a child's low chair and table. The chair has a wide curved top splat and a compound center splat in the back. The arms flare out from the back to the top of the arm supports and are pierced to receive a rod inserted to prevent the child from falling. The turned arm supports become rectangular in section at the seat rail and, as the front legs, taper on their inward sides to the floor. Probably designed to hold a moveable footrest, two holes were drilled in the front legs. The legs are strengthened by an H type stretcher. The slip seat fits into a frame formed by the seat rails. The mahogany table has a rounded top edge supported by four tapered rectangular legs connected by a simple skirt. When the chair is fastened to the table a stable highchair is formed, thus allowing a small child to sit at a standard banquet table, 28"-31" high.

Courtesy Herbert Schiffer Antiques

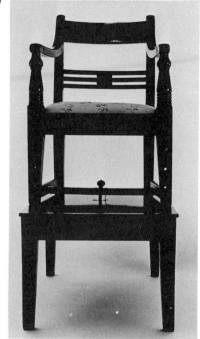

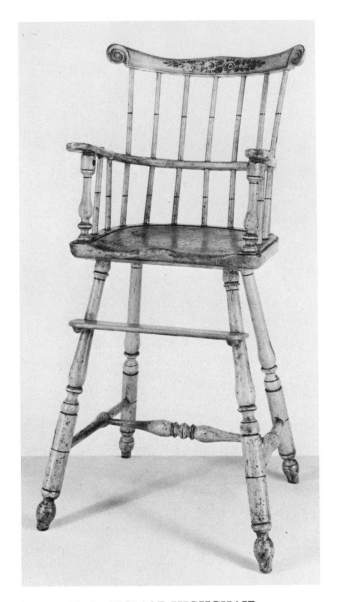

78. CHILD'S WINDSOR HIGHCHAIR

H 40¼" x W 18¼"
Pennsylvania, *c.* 1765-1810, Ash crest rail, American Red Oak center spindle, Poplar seat, Oak arm supports, Black Ash arm rail, Soft Maple legs, Yellow paint (probably not original)

This comb-back Windsor chair has a flat crest rail on which is painted a gold floral decoration. Its serpentine upper surface is flanked by generously scrolled carved ears. The crest rail is supported by seven tapered spindles. The U shaped arm rail ends in horizontally carved scrolls and is supported by elongated bulbous vase and spool turned spindles. Four long vase and ball turned legs, displaying a great deal of rake and terminating in blunt arrow feet, support the shaped saddle seat. The legs are strengthened by an H stretcher, the medial stretcher of which has a double vase and disc turning. On the two front legs, 5" below the seat, is a rectangular footrest which is rounded on the front corners. The chair is painted yellow with black striping.

Courtesy Henry Francis duPont Winterthur Museum

79. CHILD'S WINDSOR HIGHCHAIR

H 37" x W 19" x D 12"
Pennsylvania, *c.* 1750, Hickory back and spindles, Poplar seat, Maple legs and stretchers

A hoop supported by seven turned and tapered spindles forms the back of this highchair. The arms, formed from one long bent piece, are pierced by the seven back spindles and terminate in carved knuckles. The arms are supported by short turned spindles and at each end by one thick elaborately turned arm support which is pierced at the top to allow the insertion of a dowel. The chamfered and shaped seat stands on four greatly raked and crisply turned legs that are supported by a bulbously turned H stretcher. The front legs have forward extensions which hold a footrest.

Courtesy David Stockwell

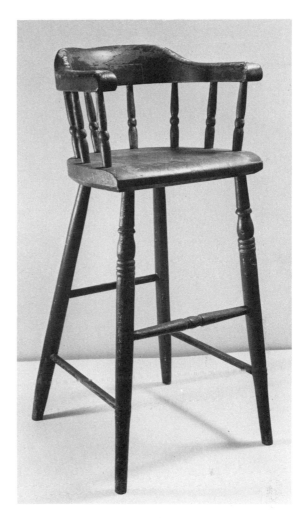

80. CHLD'S WINDSOR HIGHCHAIR

H 30¾" x W 12¾" x D 11" (Seat height 19")
Sandwich, Massachusetts, c. 1800, Hickory, Pine, Black
paint with red splotches and yellow bands

The crest rail, by curving upward in the center
while the front stretcher curves downward in the
same manner, gives additional refinement to this
bamboo turned highchair. Seven spindles form the
back. The arms terminate in turned balls, a very
unusual feature. The arm supports and stiles rake
boldly toward the center. The bamboo turned and
raked legs are connected by box stretchers. The two
stretchers connecting the front to the back legs are
lower than the two stretchers which connect front
leg to front leg and back leg to back leg. The plank
seat is nicely shaped. The chief curator of Old Sturbridge Village, Mr. Henry J. Harlow, found this
chair in the house of Samuel Wing, along with many
unfinished chair parts. These had remained in the
family until they were given to Old Sturbridge in
1965.

Courtesy Old Sturbridge Village

81. CHILD'S HIGHCHAIR

H 30¼" x W 13" x D 15"
S. C. Howe, South Gardner, Massachusetts, c. 1849,
Painted light green (original color under darker green
paint)

This chair, similar to the fireman's or captain's chair
of the Victorian era, is a product of the machine
age. The slightly arched crest rail, made of three
pieces of wood, forms the heavy arms and is supported by eight turned spindles which are decorated
by moulded ring turnings. The simple plank seat
is chamfered underneath and slopes slightly at the
front edge. The raked and tapered front legs are
turned; the back legs are simple cylinders which
taper slightly as they reach the ground. There are
two high stretchers, one which is across the front and
slightly turned with a ball, and the other which connects the back legs and is plain. Originally this chair
had a footrest just below the ornamental turning of
the front legs. Branded underneath the seat is "S.C.
Howe". *The New England Mercantile Business Di-
rectory* for 1849 lists S.S. Howe, Chair Manufacturer
of South Gardner, Mass.; if one allows for the possibility of a typographical error, Howe could have
been the maker of this chair.

Courtesy New Hampshire Historical Society

82. CHILD'S BRACE BACK CONTINUOUS ARM WINDSOR CHAIR

H 25″ (Seat height 12″)
Rhode Island, *c.* 1760, Hickory spindles, Poplar seat, Maple legs, Original green paint

This is one of the most successful children's chairs we have ever seen; it can be considered a masterpiece. The crest rail curves downward on each side to form the arms, supported by two boldly turned arm supports which are smaller versions of the legs. Other than the thirteen spindles and two braces which support the crest rail, an additional refinement of this chair is the decorative turnings which adorn the spindles, a feature seldom found on the finest of standard size chairs. The saddle seat is extremely thick and beautifully shaped with deep chamfering. Because the legs are greatly raked, the great thickness is needed to prevent the seat from splitting. The legs which have the most vigorous turnings possible are connected by a boldly turned set of H stretchers. This chair is slightly smaller than most children's chairs.

Courtesy R. T. Trump and Co., Inc.

83. CHILD'S CONTINUOUS ARM WINDSOR CHAIR

H 25″ x W 17¾″ x D 12″ (Seat height 10⅖″)
Rhode Island, *c.* 1760, Pine seat, Maple legs, Hickory spindles, Traces of green paint

Traces of its original green paint are still visible on this Windsor chair. Ten spindles and two arm supports with turnings that match those on the legs support the crest rail which is curved and bent to form the arms. To give it a feeling of lightness, the thick seat, gently dished out at the back for comfort, is chamfered both from the bottom and from the top. The well raked legs have very bold turnings and are strengthened by simple H stretchers which swell in the center. This chair was once a little longer in the legs.

Courtesy Herbert Schiffer Antiques

84. CHILD'S BOW-BACK WINDSOR ARMCHAIR

H 25″ x W (across arms) 17¾″ x D 12″ (Seat height 11¼″)
Pennsylvania, c. 1760, Hickory spindles and hoop, Maple legs, Poplar seat, Traces of old green paint

The gracefully shaped hoop that crests this chair is supported by five spindles. The arms, with applied handrests, are formed of one piece of wood that continues around the back. The turnings of the arm supports do not match those of the legs. The shaped, dished seat is extremely thick and carefully chamfered, and is supported by four vigorously vase turned and enormously raked legs. The H stretchers are simple, but bulbous in the center, an added feature in Windsor chairs. This chair has a very desirable stance.

Courtesy Mrs. Herbert F. Schiffer

86. CHILD'S FANBACK WINDSOR CHAIR

H 27″ x D 14⅜″ (Seat height 12″)
Elisha Tracy, Scotland, Connecticut, c. 1770, Original green paint later covered with yellow

This fanback Windsor chair has a crest rail with raised ears similar to the 17″ crest rail on No. 85. Two raised turned stiles flank six spindles. The deeply cut, shaped and chamfered seat rests on vigorously turned and raked legs supported by bulbous H stretchers. The chair is branded "Elisha Tracy". He lived from 1743–1809 and worked in Scotland, Connecticut.

Courtesy Herbert Schiffer Antiques

85. CHILD'S WINDSOR SIDE CHAIR

H 27″ x W 12″ x D 11¾″
Pennsylvania, c. 1770, Restored red paint

The crest rail, with raised center and ears, is similar to that on No. 86. Two boldly turned stiles flank seven spindles. (Note that the signed Tracy, No. 86, has six.) The shaped and chamfered seat is supported by vigorously cut vase and ring turned legs. The H stretchers which strengthen the legs are pleasingly bulbous in the center.

Courtesy Walter Himmelreich

86

87

87. CHILD'S COMB-BACK WINDSOR ARMCHAIR

H 30⅝″ x W 19¼″ x D 18¾″
New England, *c.* 1765, Maple legs, Oak stretcher and arms, Hickory arm supports and spindle, Ash crest rail, Tulip seat

This is an extremely rare and beautiful chair of the highest quality. The upward curving crest rail is flanked by raised curved ears and is supported by seven spindles. The arm is a continuous bent member supported by nine spindles and by boldly turned arm supports which conform to the turnings on the legs. The shaped seat is gracefully chamfered and cut away on top for comfort. Boldly turned in the ring and vase manner, the legs are strengthened by bulbous H stretchers. Both the arm supports and the legs rake outward in a characteristic manner.

Courtesy Henry Francis duPont Winterthur Museum

88. DOLL'S BRACE AND HOOP-BACK WINDSOR SIDE CHAIR

H 11¼″ x W 5½″ x D 6½″
New England, *c.* 1765, Tulip seat, Maple rear legs, Ash back brace, White Oak bow, Traces of white paint

The hoop of this chair is embellished with two gouged lines on the front surface and is supported by five spindles, two of which are braces. The deep seat is chamfered in front and supported by four bulbous turned legs strengthened by H stretchers. The initials "C.T." on the bottom may be a later addition. The presence of three spindles is quite a variation from the seven to eleven spindles found on standard size furniture. Many miniature Windsor chairs have a lesser number of spindles than their larger prototypes.

Courtesy Henry Francis duPont Winterthur Museum

89. CHILD'S WINDSOR HOOP-BACK ARMCHAIR

H 23″ x 10¾″ x D 11″
Philadelphia, *c.* 1790, Maple, Pine, Hickory, Traces of original gray paint

The hoop-back of this Windsor armchair shows considerable refinement in the two carved lines on its front edge. This hoop is supported by five tapering spindles. The arms are of the Letchworth or Philadelphia type that curl downward at the ends. Under each arm is a tapered spindle and a bamboo turned arm support very similar in character to the turnings on the legs. This type of arm, occasionally made of mahogany, is found on other Philadelphia chairs. (See Schiffer, *Furniture and Its Makers of Chester County, Pennsylvania,* ex. 68). The seat is thick, shaped and chamfered. The legs have H stretchers and are ornamented by the simplest of bamboo turnings.

Courtesy Mr. and Mrs. Edward V. Stvan

90. CHILD'S DUCKBILL WINDSOR ARMCHAIR

H 22¾″ x W 14″ x D 14″ (Seat height 10½″)
Abraham Sharpless, Chester County, Pa., 1800, Original brown paint

The crest rail and stiles of this chair are ornamented with a scratch bead. Five bamboo turned spindles support the crest rail. The Letchworth or Philadelphia type arms curve downward and terminate in carved scrolls. Under each arm is a vase turned arm support, such as those found on earlier pieces of furniture, and a bamboo turned spindle similar to the spindles on the back of the chair. The chamfered saddle seat is supported by four bold, early bamboo type legs with particularly bulbous and crisply turned stretchers. The stance of the chair is excellent. Under the seat is the inscription:
"From Ab^rm Sharpless
to
Isaac Sharpless
1800
Take care of this."
(See Schiffer, *Furniture and Its Makers of Chester County, Pennsylvania,* p. 213. Abraham Sharpless (1748–1833) is listed, but this is the first example of his work to be found. See also the standard size chair in Nutting, *Furniture Treasury,* ex. 2695.

Courtesy Peter B. Schiffer

91. CHILD'S WINDSOR SIDE CHAIR

Stamped, J. Custer, Chester County, Pa., *c.* 1798

This bird cage Windsor has a simple crest rail supported by two curved stiles. Six spindles curve backward noticeably to form the back. Two of these continue through the lower of the two parallel crest rails and join the top rail. The slightly scooped and shaped seat is supported by four legs which have a suggestion of bamboo turnings, an excellent rake, and are connected by H stretchers. The stretchers between the front and back legs are slightly bulbous. The legs are the least sophisticated of those on the examples shown thus far. (See Miller, *American Antique Furniture, A Book for Amateurs,* ex. 464. For similar standard size pieces, see Schiffer, *Furniture and Its Makers of Chester County, Pennsylvania, ex. 18, 19, 20.*)

Courtesy David Stockwell, Inc.

92

92. CHILD'S BOW-BACK WINDSOR CHAIR

H 25¾" x D 12¼" (Seat height 13")
Pennsylvania, *c.* 1810, Red paint (not original)

This child's hoop-back Windsor chair has six spindles supporting a gracefully shaped and crisply carved hoop. (See No. 79.) The seat is extremely well cut, carved and chamfered. The boldly turned and well raked legs are embellished by the best of bamboo turnings and are connected by H stretchers. (See No. 80.) This chair is signed G. Kettle (1840) but it is probably an owner's name and is certainly not the date the chair was made.

Courtesy Walter Himmelreich

93. CHILD'S FANBACK CHAIR

Measurements unavailable
J. Chestnut, Wilmington, Delaware, Early 19th century

Bamboo turnings, embellished with a line of paint in a contrasting color, form the back of this Windsor side chair. The crest rail which is curved to conform to the sitter's back is supported by the stiles and five spindles. The slightly scalloped and shaped seat rests on well raked legs strengthened by bamboo turned box stretchers. (See Bjerkoe, *The Cabinet Makers of America*, p. 63.)

Courtesy David Stockwell

94. CHILD'S BUTTERFLY WINDSOR SIDE CHAIR

H 27" (Seat height 11¼")
R. Wall, Philadelphia, Pa., *c.* 1790

Two stiles which flank seven spindles support the bamboo turned crest rail above a parallel slat. Between these two parallel rails is an oval wooden medallion flanked by two thin spindles which are continuations of spindles supporting the lower parallel member. The center spindle pierces the oval plaque or butterfly and continues to the top of the crest rail. The slightly shaped and scooped seat rests on well raked bamboo turned legs strengthened by H stretchers. A butterfly Windsor is transitional between a fancy Sheraton and a Windsor; the butterfly was often painted or decorated with some design. (See Lee, *The Ornamented Chair*, ex. 15.)

Courtesy David Stockwell

94

95

95. CHILD'S WINDSOR ARMCHAIR

H 26" x W 15" x D 15" (Seat height 12")
Philadelphia, Pa., Early 19th century, Poplar seat, Hickory spindles

A step-down crest rail, supported by six spindles, forms the back of this armchair. Each Philadelphia type arm is supported by two tapered spindles of which the front spindle is larger. (See Nutting, *Furniture Treasury*, ex. 207.) The raked legs are decorated by the least sophisticated of bamboo turnings. (Notice the difference of quality on No. 92 which could be termed the best example of bamboo turnings.) The legs are connected by bamboo turned box stretchers. (Note also the more sophisticated stretchers on No. 90.)

Courtesy John Litten

96. CHILD'S EASY CHAIR

H 38½" x W 28" x D 18½"
America, 1775–1815, Mahogany

This Chippendale chair could be taken for a full scale chair because of its perfect proportions. The crest rail is arched, the wings are beautifully chamfered and curved, and the arms are rolled. The chair stands on four legs, square in section and connected by a stretcher between both front and back legs. There is a medial stretcher and one between the back legs which flare backward.

Courtesy Henry Francis duPont Winterthur Museum

97. CHILD'S EASY CHAIR

H 35½" x W 25¼" x D 25⅜"
c. 1790–1820, Mahogany

This child's Sheraton easy chair has a serpentine crest rail, large wings and horizontally rolled arms. The rectangular rear legs are slightly tapered and curve backward. Vase elements and ring turnings decorate the front legs which terminate in short tapered feet.

Courtesy Henry Francis duPont Winterthur Museum

98. CHILD'S WING CHAIR

H 30¾″ x W 17″ x D 13″
New Hampshire, *c.* 1800

This extremely interesting and rare Hepplewhite
wing chair is the only one we have seen. The great
distance between the serpentine crest rail and the
arms is suggestive of a Martha Washington chair.
The arms terminate in stump arm supports which
turn backward and are much larger at the top than
at the bottom. The legs are heavy, square in section
and taper slightly. There is a slight backward kick
to the back legs.

CHESTS

99. CHEST OF DRAWERS

H 11½″ x W 9¾″ x D 6⅛″
New England, *c.* 1720, Pine, Original grained yellow and brown paint

This early chest of drawers has a vigorous cove moulded cornice which hides the dovetails connecting the sides to the top. There are two parallel top drawers and three full length lower drawers, all of which have plain edges and wooden knobs. The top cove moulding is repeated in reverse on the base. The case stands on four shod ball feet with slightly elongated necks.

Courtesy Mr. and Mrs. Ray Blake

100

100. MINIATURE CHEST OF DRAWERS

H 20¾″ x W 20″ x D 10¾″
Northern New England, *c.* 1730, Birch with Walnut stain; Pine (secondary)

The applied moulded top of this chest rests on a complicated and boldly executed moulding. Double arch mouldings flank the drawers vertically, but are interrupted between each drawer by a horizontal facing board with two scratch beaded mouldings. The drawers have simple fronts and very large dovetails. The drop pulls, though early, are not original. A heavy base moulding rests on the skirt which is boldly scalloped with a drop in the center. The chest is supported by bracket feet.

Courtesy Mr. and Mrs. Theodore Kapnek

UPPER LEFT NO. 21   UPPER RIGHT NO. 29

LOWER LEFT NO. 26   LOWER RIGHT NO. 30

MINIATURE NO. 23,   CHEST NO. 24

MINIATURE CLOCK NO. 155

COURTESY MRS. HERBERT F. SCHIFFER, CHEST NO. 102

101. MINIATURE CHEST OF DRAWERS

H 23½" x W 21" x D 11¾" (W at cornice 22¼")
England, 1770, Oak; Pine (secondary), Walnut drawer
sides and bottom.

The top of this William and Mary style chest of
drawers has a rounded edge. Below the overhang of
the top is a compound moulding. Plain edges, drop
pulls, and the original etched and pierced escutcheons adorn the five drawers. The escutcheons on
the two top drawers do not have locks behind the
keyholes; the three bottom drawers have replacement functioning locks. Applied half-round mouldings are on the case around each drawer. The base
moulding is a reverse of the top moulding. The feet
are formed by a continuation of the stiles. Note the

remaining part of the secret lock on the drawer in
No. 101 B. This is a feature frequently found on
early full scale Chester County furniture, but is
rarely found in miniatures and almost never found
in English furniture. This chest is seventy years later
in date than its style indicates. It is possible that it
was not made by Al Tynward Simpson, who signed
it; he might have been an owner. If this is true we
would date this piece between 1690 and 1700.

Courtesy Simon M. Warner

DETAIL NO. 101 B

102

102. MINIATURE HIGH CHEST OF DRAWERS

H 19¼" x W 16¼" x D 12¾"
Chester County, Pa., *c.* 1740, Walnut; Pine, Poplar and White Cedar (secondary)

In order to conceal the dovetail ends, a walnut board with moulded sides has been applied to the actual top of this chest. Under this applied top is a large cove moulding. The drawers which have lipped edges and very large, crude dovetailing retain some of their original 18th century drop pulls. The drawer arrangement is three short drawers in the top row over two drawers, and two long drawers above each other. The stiles extend to form the blocking for the simple bracket feet which support a heavy base moulding. This type of sturdy construction is not unusual in Chester County. The raised side panels are the most distinctive feature of this chest. Another early feature is a pair of half-round mouldings along the front edge of the sides. This piece which is put together with many pegs is extremely heavy.

Courtesy Mrs. Herbert F. Schiffer

103. CHILD'S CHEST OF DRAWERS

H 27½" x W (top) 22" x W (body) 18" x D (top) 13½" x D (body) 11"
Pennsylvania, *c.* 1750, Walnut, Poplar (secondary)

Its heavy and elaborately dentiled cornice makes this boldly designed chest of drawers particularly notable. Above the cornice is a separate piece of wood which forms a top with a vigorous moulded edge. Below the cornice is still another moulding. The unembellished drawers are ornamented by extremely large, original brasses and are arranged in the unusual fashion of two sets of short drawers over two long drawers. There is a step moulding and a convex moulding above the base which has a scalloped skirt with a center drop ornamented by a carved inverted fan. An elaborately scalloped edge decorates the bracket feet on either side of which are large dovetails. The large wooden pegs used to hold it together are a noticeable feature of this piece.

Courtesy Chester County Historical Society

104. MINIATURE HIGH CHEST OF DRAWERS

H 21¼" x W 13½" x D 10"
Southeastern Pennsylvania, *c.* 1750, Walnut, Poplar
(secondary)

Dovetailing and a complex applied moulded cornice
adorn the top of this miniature chest of drawers.
The dovetailing is very large and early in style. The
eight lipped drawers are graduated in size and are
embellished with handsome original Chippendale
brasses. A deeply cut scratch bead decorates the front
corners of the case which stands on a base moulding.
This base is a reverse of the moulded cornice and is
supported by bracket feet with unusually scalloped
inside edges. The chest is extremely heavy because
it is made of wood of the same thickness as standard
size chests. The same secret locks as those found on
many standard high chests from southeastern Pennsylvania are found on the top two tiers of drawers.
(See 101 B for remains of secret lock.)

Courtesy Mrs. J. Austin duPont

105. MINIATURE HIGH CHEST OF DRAWERS

H 13½" x W 10¼" x D 7½"
Chester County, Pennsylvania, *c.* 1760, Cherry, Poplar
(secondary)

The top of this miniature chest of drawers is
crowned by a large, deeply cut applied moulding.
The lipped drawers, arranged two small parallel
drawers over three full length drawers, have stirrup
brasses that are probably original. The front corners
of the chest are ornamented by smooth quarter
columns such as those found on Octorara furniture.
(See Schiffer, *Furniture and Its Makers of Chester
County, Pennsylvania,* exx. 146, 147, 148.) The case
rests on a simple moulding above ogee feet.

Courtesy Mrs. J. Austin duPont

106. CHILD'S OR MINIATURE
CHEST OF DRAWERS

H 25½" x W 23" x D 12½"
Philadelphia, *c.* 1760, Cherry, Poplar (secondary)

106

This is one of the most perfectly proportioned small,
quarter column chests in existence. The top edge is
surrounded by a long and complex moulding. The
drawers are graduated, lipped and embellished with
suitable, but not original brasses. Escutcheons conceal functional locks on the three long drawers,
while the two short top drawers have secret locks.
The sides have crisply cut fluted quarter columns.
Long, step, cove moulding decorates the base which
is supported by ogee feet.

Courtesy Mrs. J. Austin duPont

107. MINIATURE CHEST OF DRAWERS

Measurements unavailable
England, *c.* 1760, Mahogany, Oak (secondary)

An unusual feature of this chest is its tray top,
formed by a raised moulding applied to the front
and sides. The eight drawers, which retain their
original stirrup brass pulls, are arranged in two parallel vertical rows of four. An interesting and dainty
touch is the simple scratch beading on the dividers
between the drawers. Another unusual feature is
the fact that the sides stand forward from the drawers. The back raises to reveal eight secret drawers
arranged in the same pattern as that of the drawers
in front. The secret drawers are entirely of oak and
have a hole through which a knotted string can be
inserted to form a pull. The simple base of this chest
rests on simple bracket feet.

Courtesy Herbert Schiffer Antiques

107

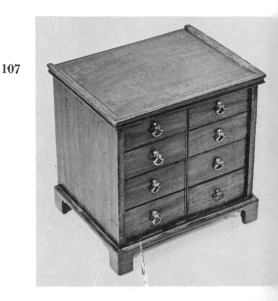

108. MINIATURE HIGH CHEST OF DRAWERS

H 26⅝″ x W 15½″ x D 11″
Lancaster, Pa., c. 1760, Walnut, Pine (secondary)

Applied mouldings above applied dentils ornament the top edges of this chest. The nine beaded edge drawers have brass pulls. Quarter columns, decorated with diagonal reeding to give the appearance of a barber pole, embellish the front corners of the chest. A bold base moulding rests on strongly cut and scrolled ogee feet.

Courtesy Mr. and Mrs. Stanley Stone

109. CHILD'S HIGH CHEST OF DRAWERS

H 20″ x W 12¼″ x D 9¾″
c. 1770, Walnut, Poplar (secondary)

This chest has a straight edged top below which is a simple moulding made with the same plane that formed the moulding above the base. There are four graduated drawers with very old brasses which are probably not original. The wood chosen for the drawer front is striped walnut. The piece stands on very simple bracket feet and is held together with large wooden pegs. The inscription on the bottom of this piece is extremely important because it may be evidence of the use of most of these miniature chest. The inscription reads, "This chest was made by your grandfather . . . (illegible) . . . Morris for your mother . . . (illegible) . . . to keep her doll's clothes." See No. 109 B which shows the back of this chest partly removed to reveal the construction and the dovetail of the drawers.

Courtesy Mrs. J. Austin duPont

109

DETAIL NO. 107

DETAIL NO. 109 B

110. MINIATURE BOWFRONT CHEST OF DRAWERS

H 17″ x W 18″ x D 9½″
Boston, *c.* 1760, Mahogany; Pine (secondary), Birch sides

This bowfront chest of drawers has a very thick top with a great deal of overhang. The veneered edges of the top conform to the curve of the case. Four graduated drawers with beaded edges are ornamented by escutcheons outlined in brass. The case rests on a vigorously moulded base above four ogee feet. The feet and brasses have been restored.

110

111

111. CHILD'S CHEST OF DRAWERS

H 25⅝″ x W 25⅞″ x D 16½″
New England, *c.* 1800–1810, Mahogany, Mahogany Veneer; White Pine (secondary)

A cove moulded edge surrounds the serpentine top of this chest. The drawers which have fronts veneered with matched crotch mahogany are decorated with beaded edges and stamped oval brasses. The base which conforms to the serpentine front is supported by long, pointed bracket feet, connected on the front and sides by an unusually curved skirt. (See Montgomery, *American Furniture, The Federal Period, 1788–1825,* Plate 146.)

Courtesy Henry Francis duPont Winterthur Museum

112. MINIATURE CHEST OF DRAWERS

H 17½" x W 14¾" x D 10¾"
Piedmont, North Carolina, c. 1800, Walnut, Yellow Pine (secondary)

A straight edge surrounds the rectangular top of this chest from North Carolina. Its four graduated drawers, whose fronts are of interesting, figured walnut, are embellished by scratch beaded edges and interior desk brasses. The diagonally reeded band on the base is reminiscent of Hackensack, New Jersey furniture. The elaborately scalloped skirt stands on delicate, tall bracket feet. Although the feet do not actually flare out at the ground, they tend to suggest French feet.

Courtesy Old Salem, Inc.

113. MINIATURE CHEST OF DRAWERS

H 11½" x W 11¾" x D 7½"
Western Pennsylvania, c. 1790, Cherry, Maple inlay; Poplar (secondary)

The front and sides of this chest are surrounded by an applied moulding. The case contains two small parallel drawers above two larger graduated drawers, all of which have scratch beaded edges and small brass desk-type pulls. The front corners have lamb's-tongues and deep chamfering as seen on No. 114. The chamfering is decorated with three vertically parallel lines of light colored maple inlay. An applied ogee moulding ornaments the lower edge of the case which rests on deeply cut ogee feet. (See *Antiques Magazine,* August 1972, p. 247.)

Courtesy John Litten

112

114. MINIATURE CHEST OF DRAWERS

H 18¾″ x W 19½″ x D 12″
Fayette County, Pennsylvania, c. 1800–1810, Walnut, Poplar (secondary)

To relieve its depth, the deeply serpentined top of this key piece of Western Pennsylvania furniture bears two lines of light colored string inlay. Rosettes and bail brasses decorate the three graduated beaded drawers, the fronts of which are brilliantly figured walnut embellished by a fine line of inlay. An unusual, but quite standard, local feature is the elongated diamond shape of the inlaid escutcheons. (See Nos. 115 and 119.) The chest has locks, but these diamonds are replacements and have not been pierced for the keyhole. The simple scalloped skirt in front, with a smaller version on the sides, is crossed by a wide band of inlay. The back feet are standard French feet formed from the side of the case. A band of light inlay outlines the skirt and continues down and around the outside of the front edge of the flared front feet which are also French. One of the most unusual features of this extremely rare, choice piece of furniture is the deeply serpentined front flanked by bold chamfering on the corners with a lamb's-tongue above and below. On this chamfered corner is a fine example of the regional specialty, the urn and vine inlay. (See Nos. 115 and 118, and *Antiques Magazine,* August 1972, p. 249.)

Courtesy John Litten

DETAIL NO. 114

110

115. MINIATURE BOWFRONT CHEST OF DRAWERS

H 17" x W 17" x D 9¼"
Western Pennsylvania, Fayette County, c. 1800–1810,
Cherry

A straight edge, ornamented with line inlay, completes this chest's top which conforms in shape to the bowfront. The inlay is in the typical Western Pennsylvania style—a line of holly stringing 1/16" from the upper and lower edges and in the center of these two lines, two curving and intercepting inlaid lines, broken only in the middle front by a light wood horizontal diamond inlay. Each graduated drawer is bordered by a band of inlay. Two lines of string inlay, well inside the edges, parallel the top of each drawer, cross the front, and are rounded at the ends. The knobs on this chest are replacements. The corners of the case are chamfered and end in lamb's-tongues at the top and bottom. The chamfer is embellished with a wavy line similar to the center of the vine inlay on many Western Pennsylvania pieces. However, this example of vine inlay is the most rudimentary in this collection. Above the base is a wide band of dark inlay flanked by two light strings. The elaborately scalloped skirt rests on rather primitive French feet.

Courtesy Mr. John Litten

DETAIL NO. 115

111

116. MINIATURE CHEST OF DRAWERS

H 16" x W 15¾" x 7¾"
Western Pennsylvania, *c.* 1800, Mahogany, Poplar (secondary)

This chest of drawers is crowned by a rectangular top surrounded on the front and sides with heavy applied moulding, beneath which is a band of light diamond inlay similar to that on No. 114. Unusually fine figured wood was used for the fronts of the four graduated beaded drawers. The pulls are picture rings and the escutcheons are simulated by inlaid wood. A chevron type of inlay decorates the chamfered front corners. French feet support a simple moulding at the base. This chest of drawers has stylistically regressed to an earlier period—Chippendale—in its construction of having a moulded edge to its top; on the other hand, it does have later—Hepplewhite—characteristics.

Courtesy Henry Francis duPont Winterthur Museum

117. MINIATURE CHEST OF DRAWERS

H 9¾" x W 10½" x D 5½"
Western Pennsylvania, *c.* 1800, Cherry, Holly and Mahogany inlay; Poplar (secondary)

This chest of drawers has an extremely thick top with veneered front and side edges, decorated with two lines of inlay. (See No. 114 for a more developed example.) Each graduated drawer front of beautifully figured cherry is bordered by one line of string inlay. The escutcheons are rounded diamonds and are not cut through. (Note the same feature on No. 114.) There have never been drawer pulls. No. 117 B shows the holes into which one must thrust a finger in order to open the drawers. The front stiles are decorated with vine inlay, a great deal less sophisticated than that shown on Nos. 114 and 115. Above the skirt, on the front and the sides, are two lines of holly inlay flanking a band of mahogany. (The sides are similar to No. 115.) The feet are continuations of the sides and the stiles. The side skirts are scalloped, while the front skirt has half an inlaid star. Each point is separated into dark and light halves. This chest, with dust-proof drawers, is the only very small piece of Western Pennsylvania inlaid furniture we have observed, and the only one to have this most unusual method of opening the drawers.

Courtesy Mrs. J. Austin duPont

DETAIL NO. 117 B.

118. MINIATURE CHEST OF DRAWERS

H 19″ x W 19¼″ x D 12″
Fayette County ,Western Pennsylvania, c, 1800, Walnut,
Poplar (secondary)

The front edge of this chest's top is embellished with a diagonal inlaid border, alternating light and dark wood to suggest rope. This same rope inlay edges the two short parallel drawers and the three full length, graduated drawers. The drawers are also embellished with a line of inlay surrounding the brasses. The same diamond shaped inlaid escutcheons on each drawer are found on the earliest and most elaborate pieces of Western Pennsylvania furniture. (See No. 114.) The skirt has a band of one-half diamond inlay, similar to the lower half of the skirt in No. 114. The stiles continue to form the turned Sheraton legs. Inlaid vines, contained within a line of simple inlay, ornament the stiles. These vines are often found in standard size pieces of Western Pennsylvania furniture such as corner cupboards, clocks, desks and chests of drawers. The sides have recessed panels.

Courtesy John Litten

119

119. MINIATURE CHEST OF DRAWERS

H 12″ x W 11″ x D 7″
Western Pennsylvania or Virginia, 1820, Mahogany, Walnut

The grain of the deep straight edges of the top of this miniature walnut chest is concealed by vertical veneers. The four graduated drawers with straight edges have brass interior desk pulls and diamond shaped inlaid escutcheons, a Western Pennsylvania feature. (See Nos. 114, 115, 118.) The back stiles are plain and, below the case, become tapered rectangular feet. The front stiles are reeded, continue past the case where they are turned, taper sharply and terminate in ball feet. The skirt is simple. The sides have flat recessed panels.

Courtesy John Litten

120. MINIATURE CHEST OF DRAWERS

H 21¼" x W 21" x D 12½"
Western Pennsylvania, *c.* 1800, Walnut, Pine (secondary)

One band of light colored string inlay decorates the flat edge of the top. Each of the five nailed drawers is decorated with a beaded edge and a border of light colored contrasting string inlay with concave curved corners. Instead of escutcheons, each has an inlay suggesting a Chippendale batwing brass escutcheon. The brasses are not original. The vigorously scalloped front skirt is decorated by an inlaid T flanked by two large commas. The boards forming the sides of the case are cut out to form a boot jack type of foot with a cutout drop between the legs. There are small pieces of wood applied to the front legs so they flare slightly forward to suggest French feet.

Courtesy Mrs. J. Austin duPont

121. MINIATURE CHEST OF DRAWERS

H 15½" x W 8¾" x D 6¾"
William Lowery, Nelson County, Kentucky, 1809, Cherry, Pine beading, Maple inlaid crescent

A complex moulding edges the top of this unusual miniature high chest of drawers which rises to a point in the center. Under this triangle is an inlaid crescent in light contrasting wood. The front corners of the case are embellished with smooth quarter columns such as those found on Octorara pieces of Pennsylvania furniture. (See Schiffer, *Furniture and Its Makers of Chester County, Pennsylvania,* pp. 146, 147.) Each of the four drawers, with cock beaded edges, has one brass interior desk pull. The case stands on a complex moulding supported by ogee feet. In a rectangular sunken field with raised letters, "William Lowery" is stamped three times on the top of the chest. The piece has a strong Pennsylvania influence. William Lowery may have worked in Philadelphia in 1800.

Courtesy of Mr. and Mrs. Laurent Jean Torno, Jr.

DETAIL NO. 121

122. CHILD'S MINIATURE HIGH CHEST OF DRAWERS

H 30¼" x W 26¼" x D 15"
Western Pennsylvania, c. 1800, Walnut, Poplar (secondary)

A scratch bead outlines the rectangular top and the eight graduated drawers of this chest. All the drawers have small brass pulls and the keyholes on the two bottom drawers are outlined in brass. The feet are formed from the sides; the outside edges of the front feet have small applied wedges, which give the feet a slight flare suggestive of a more refined French foot. A scallop next to each foot flanks the curved skirts. Although this piece is extremely simple, its perfect proportions provide it with charm and appeal.

Courtesy Mr. and Mrs. H. C. Foster

123. MINIATURE CHEST OF DRAWERS

H 13¾" x W 14" x D 7½"
Matthew Edgerton, New Brunswick, New Jersey, c. 1800, Mahogany veneer Poplar, Poplar and Holly stringing

This miniature chest of drawers is covered by a rectangular top with straight edges and some overhang. The top drawer which is deeper than the other drawers is divided into two simulated drawers by a thick line of inlay. String inlay with concave corners is found on the beaded drawers with simple brass desk pulls believed to be original. The sides and feet are of one piece of wood ending in a fanciful scallop. The deeply scalloped front skirt stands on bracket feet cut to suggest a French foot. (See Miller, *American Furniture for Amateurs*, exx. 827, 828.) Matthew Edgerton, Jr. signed several full size desks with the same disproportionately high top drawer; however, in the case of the desks, the top drawer front drops forward to serve as a writing board for the desk concealed within.

Courtesy Mrs. J. Austin duPont

124. MINIATURE CHEST OF DRAWERS AND WRITING DESK

H 12″ x W 5⅝″ x D 6⅝″
Richard Groff, Newfoundland, *c.* 1800, Mahogany, Birch and Pine (secondary)

The front edge of this chest's small rectangular top is rounded, but the side edges have been cut off to reveal the dovetails. The uppermost full length drawer is fitted for writing instruments. The drawers have simple edges and the mahogany knobs are original. The simply curved skirt of the case stands on tall bracket feet which are cut to suggest French feet, despite the fact that they do not flare out. The label reads:

> *Richard Groff No. 11 Prescott St., St. Johns NFL'D Manufacturer. Every description of plain and fancy furniture. Also turning and carving of every description . . . (illegible) . . . preparing furniture on short notice.*

This is stamped on the underside of the second drawer in purple-blue ink.

Courtesy Dr. W. M. King

125. MINIATURE MARBLE TOP CHEST OF DRAWERS

H 13″ x W 15¾″ x D 9½″
America, *c.* 1830, Mahogany

The unusual rectangular marble top of this chest has straight edges. Except for their brass knobs and large plain brass escutcheons, the three drawers are plain. To suggest the capitols of columns, the top of each front stile is ornamented with stamped brass. The front legs terminate in cuffs of the same stamped brass pattern. The back legs are not decorated. The sides of the case have flat recessed panels.

Courtesy Mrs. J. Austin duPont

126. MINIATURE CHEST OF DRAWERS

H 15″ x W 14″ x D 8″
America, c. 1800, Mahogany, Pine (secondary)

The rectangular top of this two-drawer chest has a rounded edge. Both drawers have wooden knobs, but only the upper drawer contains an escutcheon. Four bold reeds decorate the skirt. The reeded stiles are ring-turned below the case and taper into brass dog feet, such as those found on New York Sheraton and Empire furniture. (See Montgomery, *American Furniture of the Federal Period*, 1788-1825. exx. 72 and 140. Note the brass moulded front feet on the chair attributed to Duncan Phyfe. Notice also the similar reeding on the seat rail). Carved wood animal feet on French chairs were the antecedent of the New York brass examples. Occasionally New York furniture makers used carved wood for the same purpose. (See Grandjean, *Empire Furniture*, exx. 9A, 9B, and 66. Similar dog feet can be seen in exx. 5 and 51 in *Classical America, 1815–1845* published by the Newark Museum. For further information on this subject, see Miller, *American Antique Furniture, A Book for Amateurs*, Plate 235, ex. 17, and Strange, *English Furniture, Decoration, Woodwork and Applied Arts*, p. 144.)

Courtesy Miss Elizabeth D. Horne

127. MINIATURE CHEST OF DRAWERS

H 21½" x W 19½" x D 12¾"
New Hampshire, c. 1840, Original paint, Pine and Poplar

The lid of this chest of drawers lifts to reveal a till. The edges of the lid have applied mouldings. The drawers have simple edges and original wood pulls. Projecting over the other two drawers is the top drawer, supported by slightly engaged columns that terminate in turned front feet. The back legs which are square in section are a continuation of the stiles. This chest is important for its decoration. The top and sides are painted with a design probably taken from a print by Currier (before Currier's and Ive's partnership). A picture taken from an early print of Dartmouth College is inside the lid and the back has an unusual trompe l'oeil drawing of the Dartmouth Library.

Courtesy The Smithsonian Institution

128. MINIATURE CHEST OF DRAWERS

H 16″ x W 16″ x D 9¾″
Kirk and Nice, Philadelphia, *c.* 1835–1845, Mahogany veneer, Poplar (secondary)

A rectangular top with a straight edge and some overhang covers this chest. The pair of parallel top drawers, which extends out over the three graduated drawers below, is half-round in section. The drawers have plain edges and wooden knobs. Heavy engaged scrolls flanking the drawers support the overhanging top section. The sides have recessed flat panels. The back stiles continue downward to form the back feet. The front feet, unusually scrolled, are reminiscent of No. 131.   Many cabinetmakers' principle source of income was in making coffins, and some did undertaking as well. The firm of Kirk and Nice continues today as an undertaking firm.

Courtesy Germantown Historical Society

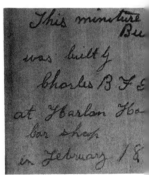

DETAIL NO. 1.

129

129. CHEST WITH LOOKING GLASS

H 9¼″ x W 9¼″ x D 6¾″ (Height including mirror 7½″)
Voegler, Philadelphia, 1836, Mahogany, Mahogany veneer; Poplar (secondary)

The rectangular looking glass is suspended by wing nuts from a pair of scrolls attached to the straight edged top of this chest. The three drawers which have plain edges, brass surrounded key holes, and glass knobs are graduated from large at the top to smaller at the bottom. The dovetailing resembles Chippendale dovetailing. The case stands on scrolled front feet (see Nos. 128 and 179) and on plain back feet which are continuations of the sides. (See Miller, *American Antique Furniture, A Book for Amateurs,* ex. 774.) The escutcheons and the key holes are visible, but there are no locks.

Courtesy Chester County Historical Society

130. MINIATURE CHEST OF DRAWERS

H 17" x W 18" x D 9"
Charles B. Smith, Wilmington, Delaware, 1837, Mahogany
veneer, Mahogany; Poplar (secondary)

The top of this chest which extends forward over
the capitols of two freestanding columns that flank
the drawers has a square edge. The capitols are
embellished by incised carving. The graduated
drawers which have plain edges that are veneered
with choice flame grain mahogany retain their original turned wooden knobs. The escutcheons are
outlined with a brass thread. The sides of the case
have flat recessed panels. There is a base that extends
beyond the case to form a seat for the bases of the
freestanding columns. Four ball feet support the
case. The inscription on this chest reads:
*This miniature bureau was built by Charles
B. F. Smith at the Holland and Hollingsworth
Car Shop in February 1837.*

Courtesy Charles G. Dorman

132. MINIATURE SERPENTINE CHEST OF DRAWERS

H 14⅜" x W 17⅛" x D 9½"
Easton, 1856, Mahogany, Mahogany veneer; Poplar and
Pine (secondary)

A rounded edge encircles the top of this miniature
chest. Its four graduated drawers, ornamented with
elongated heart shaped escutcheons of ivory or bone,
are flanked by vertically applied half-round mouldings. The feet and the corners of the case are
rounded. Just above the bracket feet is a raised applied band around the sides and front of the case.
The sides of the chest contain recessed panels. This
piece is signed: "Built by Henry Seem when an
apprentice at Sam Hogland and Dan Pitenger in
Easton—in the year 1856". This is the only piece
we have that states in writing on the case that it was
made by an apprentice.

Courtesy Yale University Art Gallery

132

131. MINIATURE CHEST OF DRAWERS

H 9¼" x W 9½" x D 5¾"
M. Watrous, Andover, Connecticut, *c.* 1850, Mahogany,
Mahogany veneer, Cherry; Pine and Poplar (secondary)

A high vertical board extends up from the back of
this chest to form the back for a pair of recessed
shallow drawers. The top of these two parallel drawers and the top over the main part of the case have
considerable overhang. The large serpentine top
drawer has no knobs. The two drawers below are
slightly set back and each has a straight front with
two large wooden knobs. The drawers are flanked

by wide serpentine stiles which terminate in crude
scroll feet. Below the case the tapered back stiles are
turned and terminate in turned ball feet. (See
Miller, *American Antique Furniture, A Book for
Amateurs,* ex. 774.) The sides of the case contain
flat sunken panels. Stenciled on the back is: "Manu-
factured by M. Watrous".

Courtesy Connecticut Historical Society

133. MINIATURE TALLBOY CHEST-ON-CHEST

H 11" x D 9" x D 5"
England, *c.* 1710, Pine, Original yellow lacquer

In the upper case of this chest are two parallel drawers above two full length drawers. A half-round moulding is applied around each drawer in the upper and lower cases. The plainly edged drawers retain their original teardrop brass cotter pin pulls and escutcheons. Quarter-round moulding is attached to the bottom of the upper case and to the base of the lower case, just above the bracket feet. An important feature of this early chest-on-chest is its retention of the original yellow lacquer decorated with gold designs.

Courtesy Mr. John Clifford

134. MINIATURE OR CHILD'S CHEST-ON-CHEST

H 42" x W (lower case) 18¾" x W (upper case) 17¼" x D 10"
Connecticut, *c.* 1750, Maple, Pine (secondary)

The proportions of this bonnet-top chest-on-chest are equal, if not superior, to any standard size piece of this type; it is a masterpiece. Vigorously and deeply cut finials embellish the bonnet which is outlined by a very heavy complex moulding. In the upper case, two small drawers flank a large center drawer decorated by an unusual carved oval sunburst. Three full length graduated drawers are also contained in the upper case. The bottom case, topped by a complex moulding, contains two full length graduated drawers over three shorter drawers. Repeating the design of the upper case, the center drawer is embellished with a carved sunburst and flanked by two plain drawers. The drawers in both the upper and lower cases are lipped and have Queen Anne type batwing brasses. The heavily moulded base rests on ogee feet flanked by glue blocks with unusually cutout volutes. (For similar feet and similar blocking see *Connecticut Furniture of the 17th and 18th Centuries,* exx, 63, 119. These are attributed to the New London area and it is felt that they were associated with the better known work of Benjamin Burnam.)

123

135. MINIATURE CHEST-ON-CHEST

H 22¾″ x W 12½″ x D 6¼″
England, *c.* 1760, Mahogany, Pine (secondary)

This miniature chest-on-chest has a very well developed complex cornice with a row of dentils, supported by a large cove moulding. The graduated lipped drawers have small picture ring pulls and Chippendale willow escutcheons which are purely decorative. In the upper case there are two parallel drawers above three full length drawers. The bottom case which has a deep moulding to receive the top case contains three full length drawers. The base moulding is supported by ogee feet.

Courtesy Mr. and Mrs. Theodore Kapnek

136. MINIATURE CHEST-ON-CHEST

H 31″ x W 15½″ x D 11″
Philadelphia, *c.* 1760, Mahogany, Pine (secondary), White Cedar drawer bottoms

A broken-arch pediment with superb heavy moulding crowns this miniature piece. Urns, surmounted by flames vigorously cut in the Philadelphia manner, ornament the three finials on fluted plinths. Both the upper and lower cases have fluted quarter columns. In the top case are four drawers; the top drawer, though carved to look like three drawers, is actually only one. An elaborate moulding conceals the juncture of the top case with the lower case, which contains two full length lipped drawers with brass desk knobs. This chest-on-chest stands on a heavy moulding and rather weak bracket feet.

Courtesy Henry Francis duPont Winterthur Museum

137. MINIATURE CHEST-ON-FRAME

H 34″ x W 21″ x D 12″
New England, *c.* 1740, Walnut

The top of this miniature chest-on-frame is outlined by a deeply moulded cornice that conforms to the chest's serpentine shape. Inlaid in a light contrasting wood on the front and separated by a primitive applied carved shell, are the initials "C G". Queen Anne brasses and escutcheons decorate the lipped drawers which are arranged two parallel drawers over two full length drawers. Each of the two top drawers has a band of diagonally grained inlay with a quarter patera in each corner. Each quarter patera is made of three pie-shaped pieces of wood inlay — one light colored section flanked by two dark sections. Two separated lines of light colored stringing embellish the two lower drawers. The case fits into a complex moulding in the frame which has a beautifully scalloped skirt inlaid with an eight-pointed star. A four-pointed star is inlaid at the top of each front leg. The legs which terminate in pad feet are deeply cabrioled with flanking glue blocks and carved shells on the knees.

Courtesy John S. Walton, Inc.

138. CHILD'S CHEST-ON-FRAME

H 32″ x W 20″ x D 9½″
Pennsylvania, *c.* 1760, Walnut, Poplar (secondary)

This chest-on-frame is capped by a bold moulding with a large center cove. The top drawer, though carved to look like three drawers, is in reality only one. The three lipped drawers are graduated in size and ornamented by brasses which are late Victorian replacements. A large moulding conceals the juncture of the chest with the frame which has vigorously scalloped cyma curves and is supported by strongly curved cabriole legs ornamented on the front knee with crisply carved shells. Volutes decorate the glue blocks which flank the knees. The legs terminate in delicate ankles with vigorously and crisply carved Philadelphia claw and ball feet. This extremely rare piece has a dust lining between the drawers and a secret catch lock under the top drawer.

Courtesy Chester County Historical Society

139. MINIATURE HIGHBOY

H 15½″ x W 6½″ x D 11¾″
Southwest Chester County, *c.* 1720, Walnut, White Oak

A stepped, thumbnail and cove moulded cornice decorates this miniature. This cove (made undoubtedly by the same moulding plane) is repeated in the moulding joint where the top and bottom cases come together. On the top case is an applied half-round moulding on the front edge and between the two pairs of small drawers over one full length drawer. The same moulding is used to decorate and outline the single drawer of the bottom case which is dovetailed. Small brass desk pulls are attached to each drawer. The skirt details, one circular curve on each side and a double cyma curve at the front, are outlined with an applied bead. The case is supported by four vigorously trumpet turned legs which are strengthened by flat box stretchers and terminate in ball feet. These stretchers curve to conform to the shaping of the front and side skirts. This refinement, the duplication of the cove moulding, and other details of design confirm this miniature William and Mary highboy as a masterpiece.

140. MINIATURE HIGHBOY

H 18″ x W 12″ x D 8″
England, *c.* 1700, Walnut, Walnut veneer on Oak, Oak drawer linings

This miniature highboy has a vigorous complex cornice. The top case contains a pair of drawers over two full length drawers, while the lower case has only one drawer. Surrounding the drawers is an applied half-round moulding on the case. The drawers have no lips or beads, but the edges are decorated with a band of diagonal veneer. The original teardrop pulls and ornately etched and curved escutcheons are over real locks. The moulding at the bottom of the top case is a reverse of the cornice, a refinement which is very unusual. The double cyma curve on the front skirt is repeated on a smaller scale on the sides. Four cabriole legs which are square in section and terminate in simple Spanish feet support the highboy.

Courtesy Mr. John Clifford

141. MINIATURE HIGHBOY

H 29″
Philadelphia, *c.* 1740, Cherry, Poplar (secondary)

A bold cornice crowns this miniature highboy. The lipped drawers are embellished by very stylishly pierced original brass pulls and escutcheons. The drawer arrangement is three parallel drawers over two paralled drawers over two full length drawers; the drawers are graduated. The lower case contains only one drawer. At the juncture of the top and bottom case is an elaborate moulding. At the sides and across the front, the skirt is made of a collection of elaborate French and cyma curves. The case stands on boldly curved cabriole legs terminating in crisply carved trifid feet.

Courtesy Mr. and Mrs. Jess Pavey

142. MINIATURE HIGHBOY

H 36⅜″ x W 26¼″ x D 13¼″
Connecticut, 1740, Cherry, Poplar and Chestnut (secondary)

The cornice of this highboy is large, coved, and complex. The upper case contains three graduated drawers; in the lower case are one full length drawer over three small drawers. The center drawer is embellished by a beautifully executed, carved fan, in the focus of which is a stirrup pull. The original willow brasses decorate each drawer. Two pendants embellish the skirt. The cabriole legs have scrolled voluted glue blocks on each side of the knees. The legs which terminate in crisp pad feet shod with sharply turned discs are slender, long and graceful.

Courtesy Henry Francis duPont Winterthur Museum

143. MINIATURE HIGHBOY

H 18" x W 10½" x D 6"
Connecticut, *c.* 1760, Walnut, Pine (secondary)

Three compressed ball and spike finials crown this miniature highboy which has a delicately curved broken-arch pediment decorated with carved rosettes. The top case contains three parallel drawers. The center drawer is embellished by a carved fan and is flanked by two drawers, the upper edges of which are shaped to conform to the curve of the pediment. Below these drawers are three graduated full length drawers. In the bottom case are three parallel drawers; the center one is ornamented with a carved fan matching that of the center top drawer. Small turned wooden knobs decorate the lipped drawers. The lower case has a vigorously cut skirt with two large cyma curve pendants ending in double-ball drops. The case stands on highly curved cabriole legs which taper to very small ankles and terminate in crisply carved pad feet. At the knees of the cabriole legs are parrot's-bill shaped glue blocks.

Courtesy Henry Francis duPont Winterthur Museum

144

144. MINIATURE HIGHBOY

H 23½" x W 15¼" x D 12"
America, Ca. 1760, Pine

The complex cornice which decorates the top of this highboy, consists of applied chevrons between two mouldings. The corners of the upper case are chamfered with lamb's-tongues above and below two lines of fluting. In the top case are two parallel drawers above two full length drawers. The base contains one drawer. Queen Anne bat-wing brasses and beaded edges embellish these graduated drawers. The complex moulding at the juncture of the top and bottom case is repeated around the base. The primitive legs of this highboy taper to small ankles and terminate in crisply carved ball and claw feet.

Courtesy Mr. and Mrs. Theodore Kapnek

129

CLOCK
INTRODUCTION

In describing and discussing miniature clocks it is necessary, in the interest of clarity, to divide the examples into two categories—floor standing clocks and table top or shelf standing clocks, This section is intended as a general survey on the subject and only a relatively small number of clocks are included.

Floor standing pieces are clocks such as dwarf tall clocks, commonly known as grandmother clocks since the Victorian Period. These are usually three and one half feet to four feet in height. It might be argued that these are not miniature, but if one compares their construction with that of tall clocks it becomes apparent that they are indeed true miniatures. The cases and movements of several clocks illustrated here were built to tall clock specifications, but in two-thirds to three-quarters scale.

Table top or shelf standing clocks are scaled down tall clocks not exceeding one foot in height. In most instances these diminutive models incorporate spring powered watch movements, rather than miniaturized weight driven tall clock movements. In some examples, the case serves as a temporary resting place for a man's watch. Some bracket clocks have watch movements permanently incorporated into their cases. The fragile nature of these pieces has made their survival quite rare.

These two categories include clocks that were made to run. An area not explored in this chapter is that of dollhouse clocks. Only the most wealthy children would have had diminutive clocks with workable movements. Most of the dollhouse scale clocks were inanimate and simply had a face painted on them. While extremely rare, a miniature clock of this description would tell us little of the society which produced it.

Consideration should be given to several points illustrated by the clocks shown here. First of all, the dwarf tall clocks must have been considered luxury items. It is unlikely that they served as the only clock in their original owner's household. Their relative scarcity indicates that they were never greatly in demand. From the illustrations here we see that they are not indicative of any region, nor are they particularly American. The one English example shown (No. 148), illustrates a dwarf tall clock of the same size as the American clocks by New England and Pennsylvania clockmakers. Earlier English clocks made in miniature scale are known, some dated

148

ENGLISH   NEW ENGLAND   PENNSYLVANIA

as early as 1700. We should assume, since there were many more clockmakers in Great Britain, that English examples of this type of clock are more numerous. One should not confuse as miniatures the North Country clocks of England, Scotland and, to a lesser extent, Ireland; some barely exceed five feet in height. They were scaled for the low ceilinged cottages of their original owners. The movements in these clocks are just as large as those in an eight or nine foot tall clock.

While the original demand for the dwarf tall clock was small, it is interesting to speculate what brought it about. There has always been an aura surrounding that which is much smaller than its counterpart. Perhaps this cuteness accounted for part of the market when a wealthy patron bought a second, or third, timepiece for his household, or for his mistress. A wealthy merchant or landowner might have had a miniature clock made for one of his children.

The original positioning of the three or four foot high dwarf tall clock is a little less certain. They are too small to have been in a formal parlor, and would have been bumped if they stood in a stair landing. Their in-between size seems to have required placement in a protected area; nevertheless, they served a purpose that may have warranted the additional expense of having them. As a bedroom clock they might have served their master well, their dial being at nearly eye level to the bed pillow. It is likely that this function was normally met by a portable bracket clock, something that is seldom encountered in America.

The regional variance in tall clock casemaking is fairly well represented here with the exception of southern and upper New Jersey and New York. Examples from those areas were not available. In the several New England dwarf clocks three definite degrees of sophistication may be seen. Three clocks by one maker, Joshua Wilder of Hingham, Massachusetts, who seems to have made a specialty of producing dwarf tall clocks as well as other more typical specimens, clearly illustrate the varying degrees of sophistication in their cases (Nos. 149, 150 and 152). Although one is made of pine once richly stained and varnished to resemble some more exotic wood such as mahogany, the two Wilder clocks at the Henry Ford Museum at Dearborn, Michigan might have been the work of the same cabinetmaker. The mouldings and turnings on the hood are similar and the overall proportions are not radically different. The clock in the painted case is a timepiece with an alarm attachment (it does not strike the hour), whereas the more sophisticated example with the light, figured mahogany veneer incorporates an eight-day striking movement housed in a very sophisticated miniaturized Roxbury, Massachusetts case. It is within the realm of possibility that one cabinetmaker made all three cases. The Winterthur dwarf tall clock by Reuben Tower, a close relative of Wilder's, shows clearly that there was sufficient demand locally for these clocks to justify another man's entering into their production.

149

150

152

151

JOSHUA WILDER   JOSHUA WILDER   JOSHUA WILDER   REUBEN TOWER

JOSHUA WILDER

In comparing the second Joshua Wilder dwarf tall clock with the Augusta, Maine example made by Nathaniel Hamlin about 1810-20 (No. 154), several interesting points should be made. The flat top with its gallery of three chimneys (in this instance all are fluted) seems to occur on New Hampshire and Maine tall clocks after 1790-1800. The fluted quarter columns (fairly wide in proportion to their height) are often encountered on Maine tall clocks. The use of pine and birch and contrasting inlays is another feature common to northern New England clocks of the early 19th century. The movement in this clock runs for eight days and strikes on the hour.

By far the most austere clock is the Benjamin Youngs timepiece made in 1810 when Youngs was under the influence of the religious group, the Shakers. Although all conscious sophistication has been dropped in favor of simplicity, the clock still retains the basic characteristics of a tall clock. Its small size enables it to be included here.

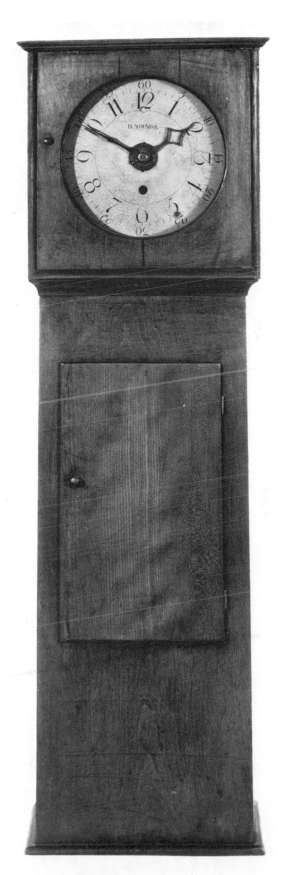

154   153

NATHANIEL HAMLIN   BENJAMIN YOUNG

137

155

156

One dwarf tall clock from Pennsylvania represents perhaps one of the finest surviving examples of the Philadelphia School at the time of the American Revolution. This curious country example is dated perhaps as late as 1830. Signed on its dial is "Hy. Bower" and "F. Swome" (No. 156). It is presumed that the former stands for Henry Bower, but the whereabouts and trade of the second man remains a mystery. Typical of Pennsylvania clocks is the rather attenuated base and hood and the broken or swan's-neck pediment, something rarely found on New England clocks. The Sheraton influence on the Bower clock is seen in the turned feet and the sunken panel on the base, as well as in the contrasting woods. These overall features are illustrated by the diminutive tall clock owned by the Chester County Historical Society. It has a watch-type movement and stands barely over thirteen inches tall. (No. 155.)

The R. Lambert dwarf tall clock, standing about three and one half feet high, is an exceptionally graceful early 19th century English example which exhibits the delicate job of miniaturization. It also has a miniaturized eight-day striking movement of high calibre.

Two of the earliest surviving American dwarf tall clocks were made by Thomas Claggett (spelled "Claget" on one dial and "Claggett" on the other) of Newport, Rhode Island. The layout of the dials, the fluted columns on the hood and the use of mahogany would indicate a later date. The scroll hood is normally encountered after 1760 in American clocks. Both of these clocks have eight-day timepiece (non-striking) movements. The Winterthur Museum specimen has some peculiarities about its dial. Not all the spandrels are original on this clock, and it is not known whether the originals were of the same design. What is most interesting is that the "X" in the figures "XI" and "XII" is engraved backward. This opens to speculation the abilities of Thomas Claggett as an engraver, and as a competent workman. Knowing his father William's keen abilities as an engraver, one wonders how such work would pass the son's approval were he as competent as his father. Comparatively few clocks by Thomas Claggett are known. It is likely that the same cabinetmaker built both cases.

THOMAS CLAGGETT   THOMAS CLAGET

CALEB LEACH

The Caleb Leach dwarf tall clock was made in 1790. It is a rather interesting miniaturization of a country New England clock. The dial, a silvered brass sheet into which the hours, numerals and signature have been engraved, is typical of the transition type of dial popular late in the 18th century before the introduction of the painted iron dial. Leach provided his dials with seconds and a calendar indication; these make this one of the most sophisticated specimens discussed here. The clock runs for eight days and strikes the hour.

Unlike the dwarf tall clocks, the diminutive sized Thomas Wagstaff London dollhouse clock owned by the Chester County Historical Society and attributed to the hand of Voegler of Philadelphia loses much in the process of miniaturization. If the movement is from the shop of Thomas Wagstaff, this may be its second case. Although somewhat crude, the case of this interesting little clock has Pennsylvania proportions, and may be linked visually with the Duffield and Bowers dwarf tall clocks mentioned above. Unlike those clocks which have miniaturized weight powered pendulum controlled movements this clock has a spring powered watch-type movement.

Miniaturization was not limited to tall clocks, but occurred sometimes in very small bracket clocks. The larger specimens are very small bracket clock cases with clock-type movements (spring powered, but pendulum controlled) while the smaller (or diminutive) styles have watch-type spring powered movements. A superb example of the first category, but not illustrated, is the Benjamin Gray London striking and repeating eight-day bracket clock in an out building at the Governor's Mansion at Colonial Williamsburg, Virginia. The case which stands less than a foot high is crammed full of highly sophisticated machinery decorated with superbly wrought engraving. The diminutive bracket clock in the Winterthur Collection (No. 157) has the signature of "Robert Wood, Philadelphia" on the dial, but has a watch-type movement of English manufacture inside. This clock most likely dates from the early 19th century, and should not be compared to the earlier Benjamin Gray London clock since the Gray clock is much more elaborate.

Clocks like the Robert Wood present a problem. They are clearly American cases with English movements of varying quality. Their delicate nature must have rendered them inoperative for the majority of their lives. Were they merely trinkets for the wealthy to enjoy? It would appear that few of these were made.

Included in this survey is another type of miniature clock, the miniature banjo clock. Clearly a takeoff on a Simon Willard patent timepiece of the 1800-1820 period, this clock cages a watch-type dial with gilt hands very similar to the early 19th century English pocket watches.

With the coming of Eli Terry's patent shelf clock in 1816, known to all as the Terry Clock, there opened another chapter in clockmaking. A machine now made pieces with interchangeable parts. While not part of this survey, it may be well to note the *c.* 1830 miniature "pillar and scroll," another name for a Terry Clock, made in Waterbury by Mark Leavenworth. The miniature steeple and beehive clocks made in Bristol and in neighboring Connecticut towns during the last half of the 19th century deserve mention. Even Chauncey Jerome's famous ogee clock of the 1840's was soon sold on a reduced scale by enterprising clockmakers bent on capturing a market untouched by the larger, full sized examples. When the first nickel plated alarm clocks were introduced, there were half scale versions offered shortly thereafter, once again proving the acceptability of the small versions. For whatever reason they were originally produced, true miniature clocks have a charm that is hard to deny.

ROBERT WOOD

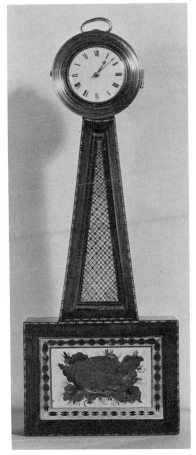

BANJO STYLE

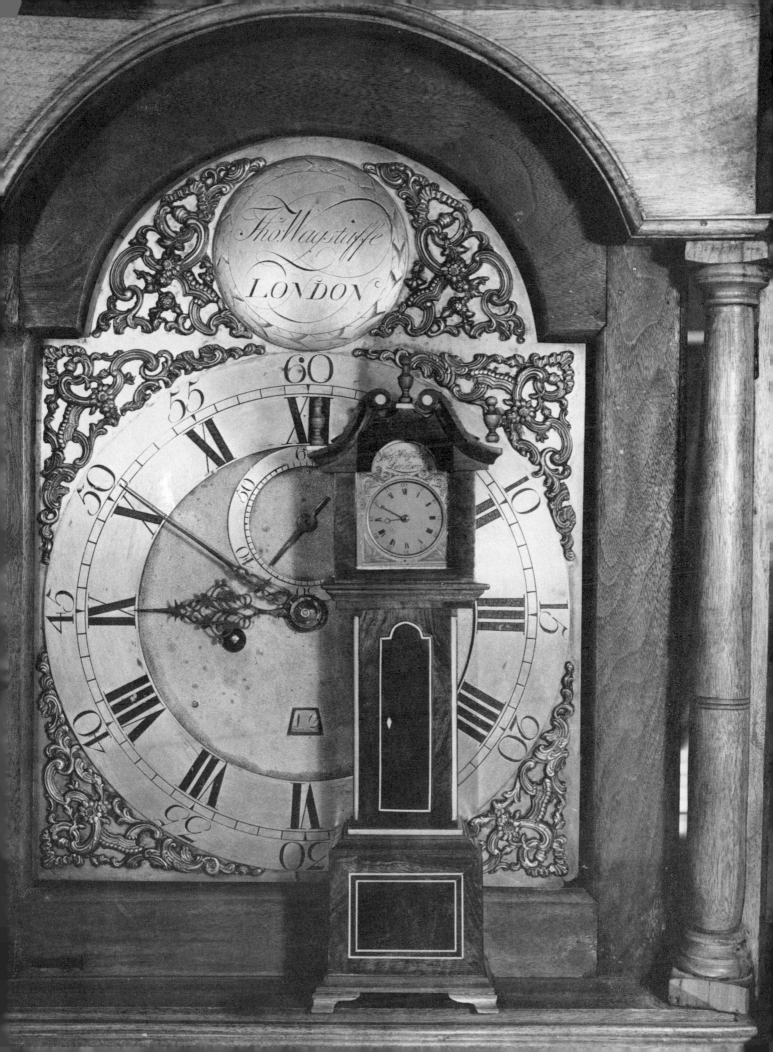

145. MINIATURE TALL CASE CLOCK

H 61"
Thomas Clagget, Newport, Rhode Island, *c.* 1760–1770,
Mahogany

Two carved urn finials with corkscrew twisted flames enhance the beauty of the broken-arch pediment of this miniature. Two freestanding fluted columns flank the door in the hood. The eight-day timepiece of this clock is very similar to that of the Winterthur specimen, No. 146. Owing to the absence of a striking section, the movement is not quite full tall clock scale. The face is brass with cast spandrels and silvered chapter rings. The top of the door in the trunk is scalloped. Beneath a moulding placed two-thirds of the distance to the floor, the base graduates into two sections which are separated by a simple moulding. Ogee feet support this clock.

Courtesy Metropolitan Museum of Art

144

146. MINIATURE OR SMALL SCALE TALL CASE CLOCK

H 66"
Thomas Claggett, Newport, Rhode Island, *c.* 1760, Mahogany

Three corkscrew flame ornamented urn finials on capped square plinths crown this clock's bonnet top. Turned rosettes decorate the broken-arch pediment. Columns flank the brass face with cast angel spandrels. The case, made of exquisitely grained mahogany, contains a door with a double curved top. The base of the clock rests on a simple base moulding.

Courtesy Henry Francis duPont Winterthur Museum

147. MINIATURE TALL CASE CLOCK

H 47½"
Caleb Leach, Plymouth, Massachusetts, *c.* 1780, Mahogany

Three brass steepletop finials on capped square plinths crown the dome of this miniature tall case clock. This clock which has a silvered engraved brass dial illustrates the transition from the earlier brass dials of the two Thomas Claggett clocks to the later painted iron dials of the clocks by Reuben Tower, Joshua Wilder and Henry Bower working in the 19th century. The hands are exceptionally ornate. The eight-day striking movement shows seconds and the date of the month. Flanking the hood are two freestanding columns in front and two engaged columns at the rear. The top of the case door conforms to the curve of the hood and face. The wide door suggests country Connecticut manufacture. Above and below the trunk are vigorous cove mouldings undoubtedly cut with the same plane. The simple base above a vigorous moulding is supported by ogee feet.

Courtesy Metropolitan Museum of Art

148. MINIATURE TALL CASE CLOCK

H 41"
R. Lambert, England, *c.* 1790–1810, Fruitwood, Ivory,
Dyed wood inlay

The bonnet of this clock is crowned by a brass urn-shaped finial flanked by swan's neck pediments adorned with applied ivory rosettes. The front of the hood is edged with two freestanding columns and under the hood is a vigorous cove moulding with a return moulding between the waist and the base. The face is painted. The door is outlined with an applied moulding; fluted quarter columns embellish the front corners of the waist. The case houses a finely wrought eight-day movement showing seconds and the date. The contrasting ivory button feet suggest Sheraton influence.

Courtesy Philip Parker

**149. JOSHUA WILDER DWARF
      TALL CASE CLOCK**

H 45"
Joshua Wilder, Hingham, Massachusetts, *c.* 1810, Mahogany, Mahogany Veneer

Housed in a straight grained mahogany and mahogany veneered case, this clock represents the intermediately priced model between the painted (or stained) soft wood case, as shown in No. 150, and the elegantly appointed example at Winterthur, No. 151. As is usual with Wilder's work, this specimen has a miniature eight-day striking tall clock movement and is of excellent quality.

Courtesy Greenfield Village and Henry Ford Museum

148

150. JOSHUA WILDER DWARF ALARM TIMEPIECE

H 43"
Joshua Wilder, Hingham, Massachusetts, *c.* 1808, Pine

Joshua Wilder, who apparently specialized in the production of dwarf timepieces and clocks, produced this specimen which has an eight-day alarm timepiece housed in a painted pine case. The finial may be a replacement.

Courtesy Greenfield Village and Henry Ford Museum

151. DWARF TALL CASE CLOCK

H 50"
Reuben Tower, Hingham, Massachusetts, *c.* 1808–1845,
Mahogany, White Pine (secondary)

The American eagle with its shield motif is typical
of the New England dials made in the early 19th
century by Samuel Curtis and Spencer Nolan at
their "dial Manufactory" in Boston. The eight-day
miniature striking movement is of finely wrought
brass and steel. Brass finials, capitals and bases on
the inset quarter columns give added elegance to
this clock.

Courtesy Henry Francis duPont Winterthur Museum

152. DWARF TALL CASE CLOCK

H 50½"
Joshua Wilder, Hingham, Massachusetts, *c.* 1815–1825,
Mahogany, White Pine (secondary)

Although it lacks the flashy brass capitals and bases
in the inset quarter columns, this clock is similar to
No. 151, the Reuben Tower dwarf tall case clock.
The choice of finely figured mahogany veneer suggests the wood normally encountered on fine Sheraton and Empire case pieces. The eight-day striking
movement is of finely wrought brass and steel. The
finish on Wilder's and Tower's movements is superb
and reflects their fine craftsmanship. (See Montgomery, *American Furniture, The Federal Period,
1788–1825*, p. 198.)

Courtesy Henry Francis duPont Winterthur Museum

151

153. SHAKER DWARF TALL CASE CLOCK

H 36″
Benjamin Youngs, Watervliet, New York, c. 1812, Pine

This eight-day timepiece is housed in a simple soft wood case which bears the signature of Benjamin Youngs, who worked near the Shaker Colony at Watervliet, New York in the early 19th century.

Courtesy Greenfield Village and Henry Ford Museum

154. DWARF TALL CASE CLOCK

H 43″
Nathaniel Hamlin, Augusta, Maine, c. 1825–1830, Walnut case, Pine (secondary), Satinwood inlay

A flat top with a reeded gallery is reflective of many of the full size clocks made in the early 19th century in northern New England. This clock has an eight-day time and striking movement showing seconds. The use of fluted quarter columns without capitols and bases is typical of many simpler New England clocks of the period.

Courtesy Greenfield Village and Henry Ford Museum

156

156. MINIATURE TALL CASE CLOCK

H 48"
Henry Bower and F. Swome, southeastern Pennsylvania,
c. 1830–1840, Maple, Poplar (secondary)

This Sheraton country clock, crowned by three
turned finials and a scroll pediment, has a case of
contrasting light wood with an inset mahogany
panel. Its proportions are similar to many clocks
made between 1820 and 1830 in southeastern Pennsylvania. The eight-day movement is finely wrought
and quite sophisticated in that it has a second hand,
date dial and phases of the moon attachment. The
corners of the trunk are chamfered and end in
lamb's-tongues. The diamond-shaped bone escutcheon is a further embellishment. The clock stands on
turned Sheraton feet. The movement and case may
have been made by Bower and Swome, respectively.
Only two other clocks of this type are known. (See
Nutting, *Furniture Treasury*, exx. 3317, 3318.) One
dial has been repainted, but all three have identical
hands. (See also Palmer, *The Book of America's
Clocks*, ex. 102.)

Courtesy William Penn Memorial Museum

155

155. WATCH CASE MADE AS MINIATURE TALL CASE CLOCK

H 13½"
Voegler, Philadelphia, Pa., c. 1836, Mahogany, Contrasting inlay

The broken-arch pediment of this clock which was
made for Voegler's dollhouse is crowned by three
urn-shaped turned finials. Instead of carved rosettes,
dots of light wood inlay embellish the pediment.
The hood rests on a bold cove moulding above a
slender waist and the door has a tombstone top outlined with a line of light contrasting inlay. The
base is ornamented with light colored string inlay
and rests on ogee feet. Above the dial is written
"Thomas Wagstaff". He was an English Quaker
clockmaker who came to America to solicit orders.
His works, shipped to America, are found in many
fine Philadelphia cases. (See Downs, *American Furniture, Queen Anne and Chippendale*, exx. 206,
207.) A Wagstaff clock case would have been made
in the Chippendale style; it is interesting to note
that this clock is translated into the Hepplewhite
idiom. Behind the finials, the top lifts out to allow
removal of the watch. The back of the watch is
engraved "Mary J. Hamilton, Philadelphia". The
key is in the case on a platform just below the watch.

Courtesy Chester County Historical Society

157. MINIATURE BRACKET CLOCK

H 9⅞"
Robert Wood, Philadelphia, *c.* 1780–1800, Mahogany

An English-made, watch-like, spring-powered movement is housed in this mahogany case. How much of this clock is American is of some question. Small clocks of this nature may have been far more common than their present scarcity suggests.

Courtesy Henry Francis duPont Winterthur Museum

158. MINIATURE BANJO CLOCK

H 12″
Boston area, *c.* 1810–1815, Mahogany, Original painted glass panels

This watch case was designed to look like a miniature banjo clock. Made largely of mahogany with contrasting bands of inlay on the front edges, the case reflects similar types that housed some of Simon Willard's early "Patent Timepieces". The movement is closely associated with watches of the late 18th and early 19th centuries. The eglomise panels are white and gold leaf, a color scheme favored by Simon Willard.

Courtesy Mr. and Mrs. Carl B. Randall

CRADLES

159. DOLL'S HOODED CRADLE

H 11¾″ x W 17″ x D 12″
Pennsylvania, Late 18th century, Pine, Painted red

Three boards form the overhanging top of this hooded cradle. The flat center board is flanked by two slanted boards. Hand holes pierce the center of each side which flares outward from the base. The top edge of the foot curves to conform to the arch of the skirt under the edge of the hood. Cheese cutter rockers support the base which protrudes beyond the sides and ends. Doll's cradles are a very common form of miniature furniture.

Courtesy Chester County Historical Society

160. DOLL'S DOUBLE CRADLE

H 18½″ x W 10-3/16″ x D 21-1/16″
New England, Late 18th century, Striped maple

This unique miniature cradle hangs from two iron rods that penetrate the serpentine top stretcher and turn at right angles to pierce the two turned posts. These urn topped posts are decorated with ring turnings; descending to meet a pair of spider feet, they become square in section and are separated by a stretcher. The cradle has two hoods, one at each end, and slats at the sides. The rails above and below the slats are dovetailed into the ends. The maple is boldly striped. (See Kirk, *Early American Furniture,* ex. 172.)

Courtesy Yale University Art Gallery   Mabel Brady Garvan Collection

161. DOLL'S CRADLE

H 10½″ x W 20″ x D 8¾″
Pennsylvania, Early 19th century, Cherry

This early cradle represents the transition from the earlier hooded cradle to the later open cradle. See No. 162.

Courtesy William Penn Memorial Museum

162. MINIATURE BABY CRIB

H 5″ x W 14″ x D 11¼″
America, Mid-19th century, Pine, Painted

The head of this crib is higher at the foot; the sides flare outward from the floor. A curved brace supports the cheese cutter rockers.

Courtesy Chester County Historical Society

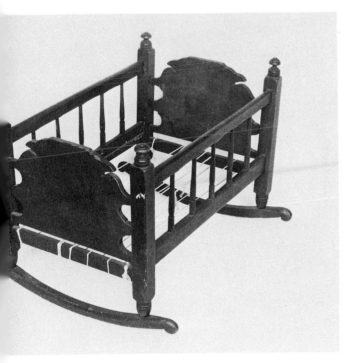

163. MINIATURE ROCKING CRIB

H 12″ x W 10½″ x D 15″
Pennsylvania, c. 1800, Mahogany

Four posts topped with crisply turned finials decorate this miniature. The posts are square in section until just before they reach the rockers where they turn and taper. The headboard and footboard are fancifully scalloped. Turned spindles separate the side and bed rails. The bottom of the crib is formed by crossed ropes on which the mattress rests.

Courtesy Mrs. J. Austin duPont

CUPBOARDS

104. MINIATURE OAK COURT CUPBOARD

H 21" x W 14" x D 5"
Wales, 1823, Oak

This miniature court cupboard is built in three sections—a top section which has a broad cornice moulding, a middle section, and a bottom section which projects forward. The back consists of a solid area embellished with a plate rail. Curved, spaced, parallel boards decorate the sides of the top section and on the front of each side is a freestanding column. The top section rests on a projecting carved cornice above a recessed area. The corners of this cornice are morticed into vertical members that end in turned drops. Below this projecting area there are three recessed tombstone paneled doors with turned wooden knobs. The sides of this section contain two raised panels. The bottom section is topped by a shelf with a step and thumbnail edge. Directly below this shelf are two parallel drawers; the front of each has a raised panel and two turned wooden pulls. Below each drawer is a raised panel door conforming to the shape of the smaller panels in the center section. A simple skirt rests on feet which are continuations of the stiles. The sides of the bottom section have a full width raised panel above two parallel vertical panels. This piece, dated 1823, was a copy of a much earlier example of furniture made about 1700.

Courtesy John Clifford

165. MINIATURE OR CHILD'S CUPBOARD

H 19″ x W 20″ x D 11″
Pennsylvania or Ohio, Mid 19th century, Pine

An applied piece of rectangular wood surrounds the side and front edges of the top of this cupboard which is painted to simulate maple veneer. To suggest a band of light inlay, the drawers, doors and panels are outlined with a line of light-colored paint. Two drawers and two cupboard doors have white porcelain knobs and flat recessed panels attached by butt hinges. The sides of the case also contain flat recessed panels. The stiles reach to the floor and taper slightly on the inside to form a suggestion of French feet.

Courtesy Mrs. J. Austin duPont

166. MINIATURE CUPBOARD

H 23½″ x W 18¼″ x D 10¾″
America, c. 1840, Pine

The rectangular top of this miniature cupboard has an overhanging rounded edge on all sides. The two parallel drawers with applied beaded edges and the flat panel cupboard doors with semi-circular tops retain their original white china knobs. Below the drawers, which are nailed, the case narrows and is decorated by mouldings embellished with pierced hearts. Below the doors which are flanked by turned columns with slanted bases and tops there is a strong base moulding above fancifully cutout feet, pierced with hearts and carpenter Gothic scallops. An unusual feature is the absence of mitering at the corners. This piece was probably painted.

Courtesy Mr. and Mrs. H. C. Foster

167. MINIATURE CUPBOARD

H 15" x W 85⁄8" x D 5"
Southern United States, 18th century, Southern Pine

This miniature cupboard is topped by a straight edged rectangular board, below which is a crude moulding. The case contains two narrow, tall doors, one above the other, flanked by raised, applied, half-round mouldings which continue over the top of each door. The doors are hung on cotter key type hinges with stirrup latches and contain boldly raised panels and a deep scribed bead around the inside edge of the wide stiles. A shallow horizontal shelf divides the doors. The cupboard rests on a simple base moulding above a straight skirt and bracket feet.

Courtesy Margaret R. Barbour

168. MINIATURE CORNER CUPBOARD

H 13¼″ x W 6¼″ x D 3¾″
Voegler, Philadelphia, Pa., 1836, Mahogany

Three urn finials crown the broken-arch pediment of this corner cupboard. The single arched door, supported by brass hinges, is glazed in the manner of many large corner cupboards and contains three shelves. (See Miller, *American Antique Furniture*, exx. 920,923.) The two paneled doors below the glass door are supported by brass hinges and contain one shelf. All three doors have brass knobs. The cupboard stands on bracket feet that are extensions of the sides.

Courtesy Chester County Historical Society

166

169. MINIATURE OR CHILD'S CORNER CUPBOARD

H 44″ x W 31¼″ x D 12″
Western Pennsylvania or Eastern Ohio, Ca. 1840, Walnut

This one-piece corner cupboard has a cove moulded cornice and two glazed doors. Below these glass doors and above the two recessed panel doors, is one drawer with simple edges. The base has an ogee moulding above bracket feet. This piece is a survival form and is much earlier in design than its date would indicate.

Courtesy Mr. and Mrs. Ken Litten

170. MINIATURE HANGING CORNER CUPBOARD

H 16½″ x W 11½″ x D 9½″
England, *c.* 1770, Mahogany

A broken-arch pediment with brass applied rosettes and a brass urn-shaped finial crowns this miniature hanging corner cupboard. The edges of the pediment and the door are decorated with a deeply cut scratch bead. The complex and heavy top mouldings suggest an earlier date than do the delicacy of the pediment and the arrangements of the panes in the door. Vertical half-round mouldings are applied at each of the four edges of the cupboard. The door is glazed in an intricate pattern similar to those in Hepplewhite's and Sheraton's design books. The interior contains scalloped shelves. The hinges and the pull are brass. A bold vigorous moulding trims the base.

Courtesy Mr. and Mrs. Theodore Kapnek

171. MINIATURE HANGING CUPBOARD

H 18¾" x W 17" x W 7¾"
England, c. 1780, Mahogany, Satinwood and Ebony inlay;
Oak (secondary)

This English cupboard with glazed doors is crowned with a delicate broken-arch pediment with applied circular rosettes. A graceful cove and step moulding outlines the pediment, under which is another bolder cove and step moulding. A band of elaborate, applied fretwork designed to form leaves and flowers further embellishes the case. A band of inlay outlines the two glazed doors which contain curving and crossing muttons. This band, similar to the inlay decorating the muttons, consists of two lines of satinwood stringing separated by a line of ebony. The interior contains two shelves. This cupboard is more refined and Hepplewhite in style than No. 170 which retains much of the heavier Chippendale influence.

Courtesy Mrs. J. Austin duPont

172. MINIATURE HANGING CUPBOARD

H 21" x W 11" x D 5¾"
England, c. 1785, Mahogany, Ebony and Satinwood veneer; Pine (secondary)

A broken-arch pediment with satinwood rosettes crowns this cupboard. The rosettes are decorated with ebony stringing outside a square of satinwood which surrounds another square of ebony. This same motif is copied at the top and bottom of the wide band of inlay that flanks the doors. The pediment is decorated with two triangles of a type of ebony and satinwood banding suggesting the herring bone work of an earlier period. The same pattern is repeated at the top and the bottom of the two glazed doors. Each door is surrounded by a wide satinwood band. Flanking these bands is a group of bands of ebony and satinwood. The muttons that divide each door into three panes are elaborately decorated with an inlay of diamond-shaped ebony on a light ground. There are two shelves that conform in height to the muttons. The base of the cupboard is surrounded by a delicate moulding.

Courtesy Mr. J. Austin duPont

173. MINIATURE DRESSER

H 28⅛″ x W 17¾″ x D 8¼″
America, *c.* 1800–1830, Pine

This pine dresser on trestle feet is extremely unsophisticated in construction. The front of the upper
section is slanted and contains three open shelves.
The base contains one shelf. This piece is a very
rare form of miniature furniture.

Courtesy Henry Francis duPont Winterthur Museum

174. MINIATURE CUPBOARD

H 45″ x W 32″ x D 11¾″
Ohio, *c.* 1840, Walnut; Cherry and Poplar (secondary)

This cupboard has a rather provincial top moulding.
Although it is a restoration, it could well be of the
original type. The doors have flat panels with butt
hinges. The moulding between the top and bottom
is very bold and early in appearance. In the community at Zoar, Ohio furniture very much in the
William and Mary tradition was made until 1850.
The brace is a restoration. The bracket feet which
have been restored are probably of the correct type,
but round Sheraton feet have been found on similar
pieces.

Courtesy John Litten

175. MINIATURE CUPBOARD-ON-CHEST

H 30¾″ x W 21¼″ x D 11½″
England, America, or West Indies, c. 1725–1750, Teak

The origin of this double-domed cupboard is an enigma. The upper case is fitted with double doors; each has an arched top and a recessed center panel and opens to reveal two long open shelves above, and two small parallel drawers below. An elaborate moulding connects the lower rectangular case to the upper case. The lower case of the cupboard which is pegged and dovetailed in front, contains two small parallel drawers and two full length drawers, all of which have pegged bottoms. An elaborate base

moulding is supported by four ogee bracket feet. There are fancifully pierced and scrolled brass escutcheons on the drawers and doors. The interior has small ring type brass pulls. The moulding, drawer back and drawer bottom are teak. It is not possible to identify the wood used for the drawer front.

Courtesy Henry Francis duPont Winterthur Museum

176. MINIATURE CUPBOARD-ON-CHEST

H 27″ x W 16¾″ x D 18½″
England, *c.* 1820, Mahogany, Oak (secondary)

A bold, heavily moulded cornice crowns this miniature cupboard-on-chest. A half-round moulding surrounds the two mirrors on the panel doors which conceal drawers in the interior. The juncture of the top and bottom cases is concealed by a moulding. The lower case contains three simple edged graduated drawers embellished by stirrup pulls and stands on a simple moulding supported by four unusual concave feet.

Courtesy Herbert Schiffer Antiques

177. MINIATURE CUPBOARD-ON-CHEST

H 18″
England, c. 1820, Mahogany, Oak (secondary)

This miniature cupboard-on-chest is crowned with a boldly moulded cornice above a flat band of vertical veneer. Below and in front of this veneer is a carved moulding suggesting flat beads and quarter-rounds on the sides. The two doors are glazed with a Gothic design and are curtained to conceal the interior drawers. Engaged turned columns with flat rectangular capitols and bases and spiraled reeding embellish the front corners. Carved flat beads enhance the half-round moulding at the juncture of the upper and lower cases. Below this moulding is a plain edged drawer containing a sunken panel edged by a smaller version of these flattened carved beads. The drawer has wooden pulls and a raised diamond-shaped escutcheon. Below the drawer, is a wide version of the flattened bead motif which continues around both sides of the case. Below this carved moulding are two doors containing sunken panels outlined by a very small version of the flattened bead carving. The engaged turned columns, ornamented with spiral reading and square capitols and bases, are repeated on the corners of the lower case. Tapered ball feet support this piece.

Courtesy C. Frederick and Son

178. CUPBOARD-ON-CHEST

H 26½″ x W 12½″ x D 8″
England, *c.* 1800, Mahogany

The straight broken pediment and cornice of this cupboard-on-chest lifts off. In the top case are two doors with recessed flat panels topped by half-round cutouts. An applied engaged column is attached to each door, inside of which are drawers with satinwood veneered fronts. The cupboard fits into a moulding on the top of the chest. The chest contains four graduated drawers; the top drawer extends out from the case, while the other three are recessed and flanked by engaged columns matching those on the cupboard top. Surrounding the base is a heavy moulding below which is a straight skirt that extends forward at each front corner to support the base of the columns and then recesses across the front of the piece.

Courtesy Mrs. J. Austin duPont

179. MINIATURE OR CHILD'S BOOKCASE

H 26½″ x W 19¼″ x D 7¾″
America, Possibly Pennsylvania, *c.* 1840, Mahogany veneer, Poplar and Pine (secondary)

Beneath the cove-moulded cornice of this bookcase are two doors, each glazed with one large pane of glass. The interior contains two shelves. The lower section contains a small drawer extending over a larger recessed drawer, flanked by scrolls which terminate in the front feet. Both drawers are ornamented with spectacular flame grain veneer. The back feet are turned.

Courtesy Mrs. J. Austin duPont

DESKS

180. CHILD'S DESK

H 26¼″ x W 23¾″ x D 14½″
New England, *c.* 1700–1735, Pine, Maple feet, Originally
painted

This desk has a long slant board above supporting slides. The interior contains a well, a short drawer, and a large drawer. Surrounding the drawers, double-arch mouldings are applied to the case. The base, decorated by a complex moulding, is supported by four unusual elongated ball feet with disproportionately long necks. The escutcheons are not original. This piece is similar in many ways to the very early blanket chests.

Courtesy Yale University Art Gallery Mabel Brady Garvan Collection

181. MINIATURE SLANT LID DESK

H 20½" x W 19½" x D 12"
Connecticut, *c.* 1720, Maple, Pine (secondary), Original
red paint

The top of this miniature desk displays dovetailing.
The interior contains six pigeon holes over three
simply edged drawers with brass pulls. Two graduated lipped drawers with William and Mary cotter
key brasses, etched back plates, and simple escutcheons are located in the lower part of the case. The
brasses which are not original have been placed
in the original holes. The slant board is held up by
simple slides. The base rests on a very complex
moulding above four crisply turned and well shod
feet.

Courtesy Mr. and Mrs. Edward B. Stvan

182. CHILD'S SLANT LID DESK

H 28¼″ x W 23¼″ x D 14½″
England, *c.* 1720–1740, Pine, Gold on original red
lacquer on raised gesso decoration

This child's desk has a narrow top and a slant board supported by two square slides. Below the slides, an applied moulding decorates the sides and front of the case. This is a survival of an earlier form in which the desk above the moulding is a separate piece. In the case, which rests on a bold moulding above simply shaped tall bracket feet, are two parallel drawers over two full length lipped drawers. A black and white picture does not do justice to the brilliant color and interesting designs on this japanned desk. (*See page 199*)

183. MINIATURE SLANT LID DESK

H 23" x W 19½" x D 11⅜"
New England, c. 1735–1840, Walnut, White pine (secondary), Cherry feet

The slant lid of this desk is supported by small slides. The desk interior contains a well and has two small pigeon holes on each side of a large center pigeon hole. Under each pair of pigeon holes is one long drawer. Some of the pigeon hole brackets are replacements. The center drawer is reverse blocked. In the lower part of the case are two lipped drawers. The interior drawers have brass desk pulls, while the drawers outside the case have etched and shaped early Queen Anne brasses secured by cotter keys. The desk stands on an elaborately moulded base supported by superbly shaped and well shod ball feet. (See Wadsworth Atheneum, *Connecticut Furniture, 17th and 18th Centuries*, exx. 171.)

Courtesy Mr. and Mrs. Mead Willis, Jr.

184. CHILD'S DESK-ON-FRAME

H 34½" x W 24" x D 13-3/16"
New England, Probably Rhode Island, c. 1700–17
Maple, Chestnut and Pine (secondary)

The slant lid of this desk conceals four small draw under pigeon holes with arched frets. Slides wh flank the top drawer support the slant board. T three graduated and lipped drawers are adorned etched Queen Anne brasses. Although they are su able, the brasses are not original. There are lo behind the escutcheons on the upper two drawe

...rame, with its fancifully scalloped skirt, stands ...ered, turned legs which terminate in shod pad ...This desk was stained red to simulate cherry. ...ad feet and the moulding at the top of the ... are painted black.

...sy Museum of Fine Arts

185. CHILD'S DESK-ON-FRAME

H 34⅛″ x W 22⅜″ x D 19⅛″
New England, *c.* 1750, Cherry, Pine (secondary)

This cherry desk-on-frame has a slant lid supported by slides. In the interior, a center section with three small drawer dividers is flanked by a pair of fret capped pigeon holes; beneath each pair of pigeon holes is a place for a drawer. All the interior drawers are missing. Two lipped drawers embellished with simple Queen Anne batwing brasses and escutcheons are located in the case. The top case fits into a very complex moulding. The frame is elaborately skirted with cyma and French curves. The cabriole legs, flanked by curved glue blocks, terminate in sharp pad feet on turned discs.

Courtesy Henry Francis duPont Winterthur Museum

186. MINIATURE KNEEHOLE DESK

H 12½″ x W 14½″ x D 9″
England, c. 1720, Mahogany, Pine and Oak (secondary)

A heavy moulded edge with considerable overhang surrounds the rectangular top of this desk. Underneath the overhang is an applied cove moulding. Complex bands of inlay border the top, the drawers and the door. The top drawer extends the entire width of the case. Situated below this drawer is a recessed cupboard flanked by three banked and graduated drawers. The drawers are ornamented by brass Queen Anne escutcheon pulls. The bales are held by bolts, rather than by cotter keys. Above the cupboard is a cyma curved skirt which is actually a drawer. The door of the cupboard is decorated by a sunburst and an inlaid crown having five points, each surmounted by a "jewel" or "boss." This light catching device is a carryover from earlier periods and is reminiscent of the decoration on fine mirrors of the period. (See Edwards, *The Shorter Dictionary of English Furniture*, ex. 22, and Wills, *English Looking Glasses, 1670-1820,* ex. 20.) The lower front corners of the case are chamfered and fluted with lamb's-tongues. A vigorous base moulding is supported by four deeply cut and unusually detailed ogee feet. To simulate drawers, mouldings and picture ring pulls are applied to the back of this desk (Plate C). (See Chippendale, *The Gentleman Cabinetmaker's Director,* **Plate CXX. 3rd Edition.**)

Courtesy Mr. and Mrs. Richard Fredericks

DETAIL NO. 186

Plate C

187. MINIATURE SLANT LID DESK

H 15½" x W 15" x D 8"
England, c. 1730, Walnut veneer on Pine fronts, Solid walnut ends, Oak interior and back, Pine drawer linings, Boxwood line inlay, Ebony veneers

In the interior of this fine desk, a center hinged door is flanked on either side by a document drawer and a pair of pigeon holes. Beneath each pair of pigeon holes is a drawer. The door is ornamented by an inlaid six-pointed star; three points are ebony and three are boxwood. Each document drawer is embellished by an engaged fluted column. Small brass interior desk pulls are on the interior drawers, on the slides that support the slant lid, and on the three parallel top drawers in the case. The veneered slant board is bordered by a band of boxwood flanked by two lines of ebony. This same decoration is repeated on the graduated drawers which have applied beaded edges. The original escutcheons are "Queen Anne" etched brasses with cotter keys holding bails. The case stands on a simple moulding above bracket feet, to which restorations have been made.

Courtesy Roger Warner

DETAIL NO. 187

184

188. MINIATURE SLANT LID DESK

H 22½" x W 21" x D 11⅜"
North Carolina, 1756, Walnut, White Pine (secondary)

The interior of this miniature walnut slant front desk is divided into pigeon holes and drawers. Two document drawers flank a pigeon hole and drawer in the center section. Flanking each document drawer is a pair of pigeon holes and a drawer. The outside drawers and the slides which support the slant lid are surrounded on the case by double-arched mouldings. The three graduated drawers retain their original Queen Anne brass cotter key pulls and escutcheons. Tall bracket feet with cyma curve edges support the case which rests on a bold ogee moulding. (See No. 100) Although it is dated 1756, this desk is nearer in style to the year 1720.

DETAIL NO. 188

185

189

189. MINIATURE DESK-ON-FRAME

H 18½″ x W 15″ x D 8″
New England, *c.* 1760, Cherry, Chestnut (secondary)

The steep slant board of this desk has breadboard ends and is supported by simple slides. Fanciful fretted pigeon holes and French curved dividers contribute to the interesting interior. Beneath each pair of pigeon holes is a drawer with standard brass interior drawer pulls. The same type of pull is used on the three graduated and lipped exterior drawers. The remarkable feature of this miniature is its separate base. A deep cove moulding conceals the juncture of the frame and the case. Alternating French curves form a pendant in the center of the skirt. The piece rests on elaborately cutout bracket feet, on the outside of which dovetails are visible.

Courtesy Mr. and Mrs. Theodore Kapnek

DETAIL NO. 189

191. MINIATURE OR DOLL'S SLANT LID DESK

H 11" x W 8⅞" x D 4¾"
England, *c.* 1780, Mahogany, Chestnut and Oak (secondary)

A steep slant board, supported by two small slides, conceals four fretted pigeon holes and three drawers in the interior. Inside, the slant board is inlaid with a replaced leather pad; on the outside of the slant board, a line of inlay, consisting of dark, light and medium rectangles placed end to end, forms a border. This same inlay is repeated on the drawers. The three graduated drawers in the exterior are dovetailed. A delicate moulding, supported by small refined bracket feet, forms the base of this piece.

Courtesy Herbert Schiffer Antiques

191

190. CHILD'S SLANT LID DESK

H 30¾" x W 28" x D 16"
New England, *c.* 1760, Pine, Traces of paint

This desk contains three graduated and lipped drawers with Chippendale brasses and escutcheons which do not conceal locks. Simple slides with lipped edges support the slant board. The case stands on a bold ogee moulding on tall bracket feet.

Courtesy Yale University Art Gallery, Mable Grady Garvin Collection

DETAIL NO. 191

192. MINIATURE SLANT LID DESK

H 11⅜″ x W 16⅝″ x D 9¼″
Charleston, South Carolina, c. 1800, Mahogany; Pine and
Poplar (secondary)

The outside of the slant lid, the slides that support
it, and the drawers are outlined by a string of light
wood inlay. The interior, consisting of six pigeon
holes, is concealed by the slant lid. The interior
drawers are plainly edged and have simple brass
pulls. Light wood string inlay decorates the four
graduated drawers which are adorned by large brass
desk pulls and escutcheons outlined by a brass
thread. Two parallel lines of string inlay cross the
front of the base. Each scalloped side, formed from
one board, has a boot jack end. The case which is
embellished by a scalloped front skirt stands on restored French feet.

Courtesy Museum of Southern Decorative Arts

DETAIL N●

193. MINIATURE OR CHILD'S CYLINDER-FALL FRONT DESK

H 16½″ x W 15″ x D 8″

This high quality and beautifully executed Hepplewhite cylinder-fall front desk is decorated by a line
of rope inlay around the front edge of the top and
along the outside edge of the case. The cylindrical
desk cover is inlaid with a large shell in a dark oval.
This oval is set in a larger oval background; the
entire decoration is outlined by a complicated line
of light colored string inlay with deeply indented
corners. This design is repeated on each of the three
graduated drawers. Each drawer has two picture ring
pulls (See Chippendale, *The Gentleman and Cabinetmaker's Director*, Plate CXX.) and an inlaid
escutcheon outlined by a string of light colored wood
in the balloon shape which is a Baltimore characteristic. (See Montgomery, *American Furniture, The
Federal Period, 1788–1825*, fig. 127.) The escutcheons
are not pierced for locks. The typical Baltimore serpentine etched skirt is enhanced by a half-round
drop, in the middle of which is a strange asymetrical
inlay suggesting ferns. (See Montgomery, *American
Furniture of the Federal Period, 1788–1825*, p. 184.)
This piece stands on French feet of the greatest delicacy, height and refinement. Late eighteenth century
American desks with cylinder-falls are rarely found
in the standard size; miniature versions are incredi-
bly difficult to find.

Courtesy Henry Francis duPont Winterthur Museum

193

194. MINIATURE SLANT LID DESK

H 8¾" x W 7½" x D 3⅝"
England (?), *c.* 1816–1818, Mahogany, Brown and red paint; White and Red Pine (secondary)

An escutcheon with keyhole and lock embellishes this desk's slant board which is supported by two simple slides. The three graduated drawers have small brass interior desk pulls and large cutout brass Chippendale style escutcheons with no locks. Tall graceful bracket feet support this piece which has a straight skirt. The most important feature of this desk is its label which reads: "Abraham Forst, July 4, 1816." On the edge of the label is printed "Anderson and Mechan, Printers" and "100 Cherry Street." This address indicates that the desk had a Philadelphia association.

Courtesy Henry Francis duPont Winterthur Museum

194

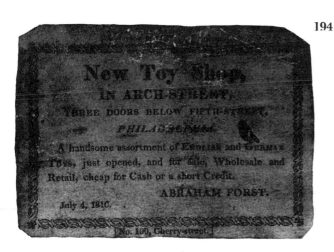

DETAIL NO. 194

195. MINIATURE DESK AND BOOKCASE

H 30" x W 13" x D 18"
Pennsylvania, *c.* 1750, Cherry, Poplar (secondary)

Deeply coved and complex moulded corners top this miniature secretary whose doors are embellished by raised tombstone panels. The interior contains a pigeonhole flanked by two tiers of three drawers. Small slides support the slant board. The three graduated drawers have Chippendale escutcheons and pulls. A wide moulding surrounds the base which is supported by bracket feet. This desk and bookcase is made in one piece.

Courtesy David Stockwell, Inc.

197. MINIATURE DESK AND BOOKCASE

H 23¾″ x W 11¾″ x D 7¼″ (Writing height 8½″)
England, c. 1750, Walnut, Walnut veneer; Oak (secondary)

The top of this miniature secretary is ornamented with a bold ogee moulding. The two doors have an applied half-round moulding which surrounds the glazing and rises to a cyma curve. The upper case contains two shelves. No moulding conceals the juncture of the upper and lower cases. The slant lid, supported by two slides, conceals a stepped and blocked interior. A vigorous moulding matches the moulding of the cornice and surrounds the base which is supported by unusually cut and shaped bracket feet.

Courtesy Mr. and Mrs. Theodore Kapnek

197

196. MINIATURE LACQUERED DESK AND BOOKCASE

H 30⅛″ x W 30¼″ x D 9¾″
China for American or English market, c. 1740, Spruce and White Pine, Black lacquer and gold leaf

A crowned eagle on a central plinth stands above the broken scroll pediment. The rectangular upper case with double paneled doors conceals a paneled interior with upper and lower drawers separated by a large removable central cupboard unit of shelves and compartments. The removal of the center compartment reveals banks of three drawers on either side. The slide supported front writing area opens to reveal an interior fitted with small drawers and compartments. The one large drawer in the lower case has a brass drop pull and an escutcheon. Black lacquer, embellished with elaborate gold leaf oriental landscapes and floral forms, covers the exterior and most of the interior surfaces. Small brass bail handles are visible on either side of the lower case which is supported on a frame with straight bracket feet. Many of the drawers exhibit an oriental character on their back outer surfaces.

Courtesy Henry Francis duPont Winterthur Museum

191

DETAIL NO. 198

198. MINIATURE CYLINDER-FALL
DESK AND BOOKCASE

H 25¾" x W 10½" x D 11½"
England, *c.* 1800, Mahogany; Oak (secondary)

This unusual miniature secretary has a bold complex cornice. In the upper case which lifts off the lower case, are a pair of parallel, graduated drawers over three full length drawers. These drawers are decorated by beaded edges and turned knobs of ivory. The interior's cylindrical cover is covered with an elaborate basket weave pattern in contrasting veneers. Curved to conform to the cylindrical cover, the interior drawers are decorated with string inlay surrounded by veneered satinwood bands on the case. The drawer in the lower case conforms to those in the upper case. Added refinements are the cornice moulding, the moulding at the top of the bottom case and the moulding on the base. These mouldings are of exactly the same design, but of different sizes. The elaborately scrolled skirt rests on bracket feet.

Courtesy Mr. and Mrs. Theodore Kapnek

192

199. MINIATURE DESK AND BOOKCASE

H 26" x W 10¼" x D 7"
England, *c.* 1780, Mahogany, Mahogany veneer; Oak (secondary)

A spherical finial crowns the center of the broken, straight pediment of this secretary. Fifteen panes are contained within each of the glazed doors. The muttons are made in much the same manner as those on a standard size piece. There are four shelves in the interior of the upper case. The slant lid, supported by simple slides, opens to reveal a small center cupboard flanked by four pigeon holes over two banks of two drawers. The bottom case also contains four graduated drawers with scratch beaded edges. All the drawers are equipped with turned ivory knobs. A scalloped skirt surrounds the base which stands on daintily shaped French feet.

Courtesy Mr. and Mrs. Theodore Kapnek

200. MINIATURE DESK AND BOOKCASE

H 11" x W 8¼" x D 5"
M. Watrous, Andover, Connecticut, *c.* 1840, Cherry, Touches of original red paint; Pine (secondary)

This miniature desk and bookcase has a deeply cut moulded top above two doors glazed with clear glass. Each Gothic glass panel is arched and swings on simple butt hinges. The drawer has plain edges and wooden knobs. The front skirt is straight. The sides are made of one board and are cut out to form the feet in a fanciful boot jack type end. The front feet are similar to those on No. 128.

Courtesy Mrs. E. M. Hartman

201. MINIATURE DESK AND BOOKCASE

H 26″ x W 14¾″ x D 7″
New England, *c.* 1810, White Pine with original reddish stain

This rare miniature Sheraton secretary has a bonnet top with a delicate pediment. At each corner is a fluted and capped square plinth which is topped by a ball and tapered spike finial. The center plinth shows no sign of ever having supported an ornament. Below the bonnet is a moulded cornice. The doors in the top case have reeded mouldings visible on the outside edges. The same moulding simulates panels by a rectangular outline applied to the centers of the doors. Below the doors there are two drawers with applied beaded edges. The top case is contained by a moulding applied to the lower case. In the lower case are slides to support the slant board and three nailed drawers with applied beaded edges. The slant board retains its original pink velvet fabric. An applied moulding surrounds the edge of the straight skirt. This piece stands on Sheraton turned feet. Except for the finials and the top brasses on the door, this miniature is original.

Courtesy Herbert Schiffer Antiques

202. MINIATURE DESK AND BOOKCASE

H (to top of finial) 49½″
Pennsylvania, c. 1790, Walnut, Mahogany finials, Maple
inlay; Poplar (secondary)

The bonnet top of this desk and bookcase is outlined by a bold moulding. The front of the center
finial is flattened and inlaid with contrasting light
and dark wood veneers in a pattern suggestive of
a maltese cross. A smaller version of the same pattern is employed on the rosettes. Below the center
plinth is an oval inlaid patera using the same contrasting woods. The edge of the platform on the
center plinth is inlaid with alternate light and dark
squares of wood. The two side finials stand on
reeded smokestack plinths decorated with the same
alternate light and dark inlay. These finials are
very similar in shape to the brass finials found on
Terry clocks, but are made of mahogany with vertically inlaid lines. Underneath the bonnet, a flat
band of alternate light and dark inlay suggests
dentiling. The outside edge of each wooden door
is outlined with a band of light contrasting stringing. The inside of the stiles which contain a panel
of flame grained walnut is also outlined by a line
of light contrasting wood. A darker band and a
cock beaded edge further embellish the outside of
the two doors. The keyholes in the doors have brass
inserts for escutcheons. The bookcase stands on the
top of the base which is rectangular and straight
edged with some overhang. In the base are four
graduated drawers; each is outlined with applied
cock beading and a border of light contrasting
stringing. There are two pressed brass pulls on
each drawer. The top drawer pulls out to reveal a
desk interior. The lower case, supported by French
feet, is embellished by a scalloped skirt.

Courtesy Greenfield Village and Henry Ford Museum

LOOKING GLASSES

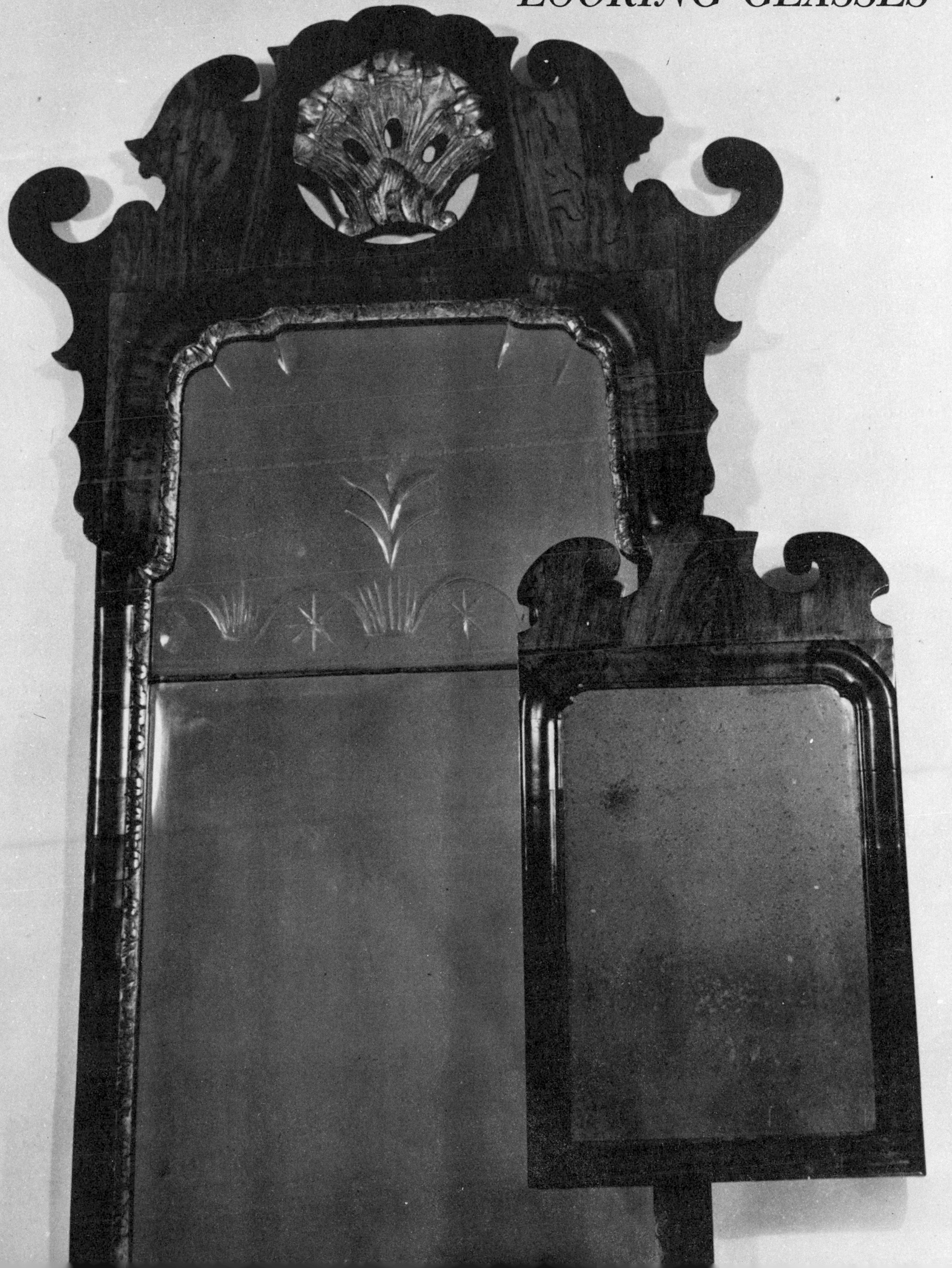

203. DOLL'S LOOKING GLASS (One of a Pair)

H 9½″ x W 6¼″
England, *c.* 1725, Walnut

Crisply carved Baroque looking glasses are particularly interesting in that many of their details, such as cabochons, deeply ribbed and swirled leaves, and piercing, are elements that continue into the rococo and are placed asymmetrically in *The Gentleman and Cabinet Maker's Director* by Chippendale. (See Plate CLXVII.) This plate shows many of the same tricks of design as in the Dover publication reprint, Plate 5; this looking glass, inspired by Plate CLXVII, shows many of the same carver's tricks particularly at its corners. (See also Wills, *English Looking Glasses 1670–1820,* Plate 61.)

Courtesy Mr. Philip Parker

204. MINIATURE LOOKING GLASS

H 17¼″ x W 10″
Walnut, Walnut veneer; Pine (secondary)

The scrolled and cutout top and high crest of this looking glass can be seen in Nutting's *Furniture Treasury,* exx. 2836 and 2863. Curved and slightly notched corners embellish the moulding of the frame. Such corners are typical of the looking glasses from 1740 to 1760, after which the frames surrounding looking glasses tended to be square at the upper corners. The glass itself, obviously period, is not beveled as are the finest examples. (See Sack, *Fine Points of Furniture, Early American,* p. 202.)

Courtesy Mr. and Mrs. Theodore Kapnek

COURTESY GREENFIELD VILLAGE AND HENRY FORD MUSEUM

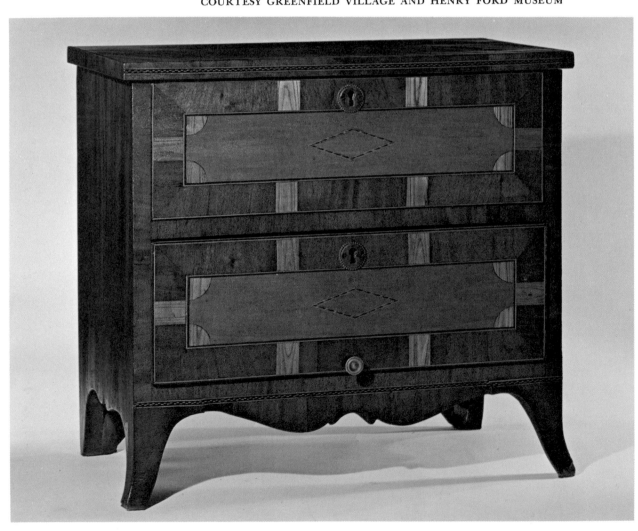

CHEST NO. 32

205. MINIATURE OR DOLL'S JAPANNED SHAVING GLASS

H 22½" x W 7⅝" x D 3"
England, *c.* 1720, Black and gold lacquer

The simple yet sophisticated crest of this shaving glass is formed by a series of reverse curves. The moulding, of the bold bolection type, would match some of those used on mantle and chimney surrounds of the period. The posts which support the glass have very bold early turnings, and are connected to the glass with wing nuts. The posts are attached to the case by trestles which remind one that this is a very early piece of furniture. The case is stepped and the simply edged drawers are surrounded by raised, half-round mouldings. The feet are simple bracket feet. This is one of the rarest and most charming miniatures we have had the pleasure of examining. (See Wills, *English Looking Glasses 1670–1820*, ex. 8, and Edwards, *The Shorter Dictionary of English Furniture*, ex. 8.)

Courtesy Victoria and Albert Museum

206. MINIATURE SHAVING MIRROR OR CHEVAL GLASS

H 8¾" x W 5¾"
America, 19th century, Mahogany

This looking glass has a rounded top with straight sides and bottom framed at the inner edge by thin lines of brass. The supports which stand on trestle feet exhibit bold vase rings and sausage turnings. The cross stretcher has turnings of a double urn and ball type, ornamented with more than the usual number of discs. The cross stretcher is similar in style to the front stretchers on the best of slat-back chairs of an earlier period.

Courtesy Henry Francis duPont Winterthur Museum

207. MINIATURE LOOKING GLASS

H 8⅞″ x W 5½″
America, Early 19th century, Mahogany

A scalloped and scrolled top and bottom, each flanked by a pair of ears curved inward, adorn the rectangular moulding of this glass. This glass is similar to many looking glasses made in Pennsylvania and New England during the early 19th century. Note the similarity of the looking glasses in exx. 221, 222, and 223 in Montgomery, *American Furniture, The Federal Period, 1788–1825.*

Courtesy Henry Francis duPont Winterthur Museum

208. MINIATURE LOOKING GLASS

H 14″ x W (extreme) 8″
America, *c.* 1810, Gold leaf on Pine

This miniature rectangular Sheraton looking glass is far more developed and ornate than No. 209. The top corners are deepest above the two sides of the frame; pendant acorns decorate the complex top moulding which is recessed in the center. The raised blocks are decorated with applied leaves. Applied columns that continue to the raised corner blocks are decorated with elongated capitals and turned discs. A group of mouldings is situated between the lower corner blocks which are decorated by applied flowers. The glass is separated, at the top, into a smaller eglomise panel embellished at each corner by two bunches of grapes around an oval center featuring an eagle. The lower glass is not decorated. The base moulding, though smaller than the cornice moulding, is also recessed in the center. (See Montgomery, *American Furniture, The Federal Period, 1788–1825,* exx. 239, 240. The standard size looking glasses shown use balls instead of acorns. The oval spandrel containing the eagle could have been inspired by 241.)

Courtesy Mrs. J. Austin duPont

209. MINIATURE LOOKING GLASS

H 11½″ x W 19⅛– x D 2¼″
England or America, *c.* 1815–1840, Gold leaf over pine

The top of this rectangular looking glass is ornamented with a boldly overhanging cornice embellished by pendant balls. The cornice extends
forward at the two sides, but recedes in the center
to contrast with the two raised rectangular corner
blocks. A rope moulding forms the sides of the
frame. A raised half spindle moulding, applied to
the bottom frame and decorated by a pattern of
turned discs, connects the two square raised corner
blocks. A gold leafed moulding may have covered
the juncture of the upper and lower mirrors. (See
Montgomery, *American Furniture, The Federal
Period, 1788–1825,* exx. 239, 240.)

Courtesy Henry Francis duPont Winterthur Museum

210. MINIATURE CONVEX MIRROR

Diameter 5″
England, *c.* 1800, Brass

Brass balls decorate this extremely rare miniature
convex mirror. The original glass is perfectly
rounded and gives no distortion to the reflection.
A more sophisticated and highly developed standard size convex mirror may be seen in Wills,
English Looking Glasses 1670–1820, ex. 163.

Courtesy Mr. Philip Parker

POLE SCREENS

211. MINIATURE POLE SCREEN

H 21″ x W 7½″
England, *c.* 1770, Mahogany

A turned post rising from a vase turning supports this oval adjustable screen which consists of a single board. Its cabriole legs descend to dolphin head feet. Many of the pieces in this book presented a problem of selection; in some cases the illustration was chosen from fifty or more examples. Pole screens are a type of miniature for which there were few examples. This particular screen handles extremely well; its age and authenticity are obvious from its shrinkage, color, and chisel marks.

Courtesy Mr. and Mrs. Theodore Kapnek

212. MINIATURE POLE SCREEN

H 18″ x W 6¼″
England, *c.* 1780, Mahogany

The top of this pole is ornamented by a turned ball. The adjustable screen is painted to simulate a frame with a needlework center. Three snake legs which terminate in crisply cut spade feet support the delicate vase turned pedestal.

Courtesy Mrs. J. Austin duPont

213. DOLL'S HOUSE POLE SCREEN

H 8¼″ x W 3½″
Voegler, Philadelphia, 1836, Mahogany and Brass

A brass rod supports this movable screen which is formed by a mahogany octagonal frame containing needlework. At the bottom of the brass rod is a glass bead. The triangular mahogany pedestal stands on a three sided base supported by primitive scroll feet.

Courtesy Chester County Historical Society

SHELVES

214. MINIATURE OPEN HANGING SHELVES

H 8¾" x W 7½" x D 2⅞"
America, *c.* Early 19th century, Walnut

Because the bottom shelf is deeper than the two
shelves above it, the sides of this miniature hanging
shelf increase in width at the bottom. Plate rails
are situated above and in front of the two top
shelves. The plate rails and shelves are mortised
into the sides.

Courtesy Greenfield Village and Henry Ford Museum

215. MINIATURE OR DOLL'S HANGING SHELVES

H 9½" x W 5¾" x D 2"
England, *c.* 1760, Mahogany, Oak (secondary)

This is perhaps the most perfectly executed and successfully designed piece of miniature furniture discussed in this book. These four extremely thin graduated shelves have straight front edges. The sides are pierced and carved in masterly fashion. The drawers are exquisitely dovetailed and enhanced by their original ivory knobs. Standard size hanging shelves of this quality, authenticity and refinement are rare.

Courtesy Miss Natalie Fredericks

ACTUAL SIZE

SIDEBOARDS

216. MINIATURE SIDEBOARD
OR CUPBOARD

H 11¼″ x W 23¼″ x D 12″
French Canada, *c.* 1780, Walnut, Poplar (secondary)

The rectangular top of this cupboard has a straight
edge. A recessed flat panel door is flanked on either
side by a bank of four drawers. The upper and
lower edges of the drawers are ornamented by
scratch beads. An applied half-round moulding
covers the juncture of the bottom of the case and
the leg. The case is supported on four gracefully
curved cabriole legs terminating in slipper feet.
The unusual thickness of the sides of the drawers
and of the entire case makes this piece exceedingly
heavy.

Courtesy Mrs. J. Austin duPont

217. MINIATURE SIDEBOARD

H 16⅜″ x W 22⅜″ x D 9⅝″
New England, 1780–1800, Mahogany; Ebony and light
wood stringing, Ebony cuffs; Pine (secondary)

A line of string inlay decorates the thick edge of
the top of this sideboard. The top conforms to the
shape of the case which exhibits a swelled center
section flanked by concave ends. Except for the
center top drawer which has small brass knobs,
the beaded edge drawers have stirrup pulls. All the
drawers are decorated by wide bands of inlay and
a band of stringing embellishes the skirt. A vertical
rectangle, convex at the top and concave at the
bottom, is inlaid in each of the front stiles. To
suggest bell flowers, the outline pattern on the legs
turns down to three drops. The cuffs, consisting of
two light lines separated by a band of darker inlay,
are a further embellishment. The cuffs are only on
the front and sides of the legs. Below the cuffs, the
legs taper more strongly. These legs are unusually
tall and graceful for a miniature piece.

Courtesy Henry Francis duPont Winterthur Museum

218. MINIATURE SIDEBOARD

H 9" x W 14½" x D 7½"
Massachusetts or Connecticut, *c.* 1800, Mahogany, Long-
leaf Pine (secondary)

The top of this miniature serpentined sideboard is straight edged and ornamented in front with bold inlay consisting of a line top and bottom separated by vertical alternating bands of light and dark inlay. The drawers have simple edges and large punched brass pulls of the period. The skirt is decorated with a band of complicated Massachusetts type inlay. The legs are embellished by a branch with leaves above a rudimentary shield with bold vertical stripes. Below this and above a cuff decorated with the same inlay found on the skirt, is a line inlay surrounding a pendant bell flower. (See Montgomery, *American Furniture, The Federal Period, 1788–1825*. The inlay on the skirt and cuff is similar to ex. 26. The sprig of flowers on the legs suggests ex. 92. Ex. 286, the New York City card table, shows a similar inlay.) While this example is heavier in outline and design than a scale model, the great vigor of the inlay and the ingenious use of the serpentine front give this unusual primitive great charm.

DETAIL NO. 218

ACTUAL SIZE

218

215

219. MINIATURE SIDEBOARD

H 10¾″ x W 18⅞″ x D 4½″
James Curtis, New York, 1823, Mahogany; Mahogany,
Pine, and Striped Maple (secondary)

Two banks of four straight fronted drawers flank a wider bow-front center section in the case of this sideboard. The top drawers are more than twice as high as the other graduated drawers. The top center drawer has a large contrasting wood veneer diamond inlaid between the pulls. The drawers have plain edges, unusually fine quality dovetailing, and their original punched brass pulls. The lower edge of the case is decorated by a half-round moulding which matches the edge of the top. Six short turned Sheraton legs, decorated by a group of disc turnings, terminate in turned ball feet. Among the unusual features of this sideboard are the use of striped maple and a variety of other woods not usually used for drawer sides, the signature, date, and the most extraordinary idea of practicing inlay patterns on the sides of the drawers.

Courtesy Henry Francis duPont Winterthur Museum

DETAIL NO. 219

COURTESY GREENFIELD VILLAGE AND HENRY FORD MUSEUM, DESK NO. 202

COURTESY HENRY FRANCIS DU PONT WINTHERTHUR MUSEUM

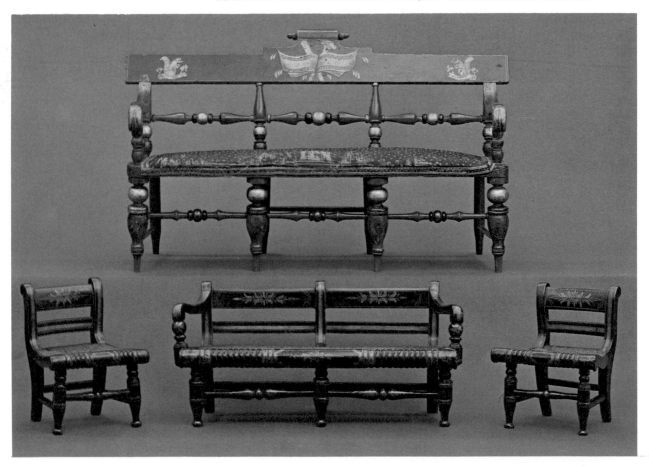

TOP SETTEE NO. 229   BOTTOM SETTEE AND CHAIRS NO. 228

218

220. MINIATURE SIDEBOARD

H 10⅜″ x W 11⅝″ x D 5½″
America, 1800–1840, Striped maple veneer, Ebony stringing, Cherry veneer, drawer fronts, Mahogany legs; Poplar
(secondary)

This miniature semi-circular sideboard has a plain
top with straight edges. The front of the case is
divided by two front legs into three sections. The
legs are half-round in section, become disc turned,
and taper through vase turnings to the floor. The
center panel contains three black edged graduated
drawers, each embellished with one turned wooden
knob. This is an extremely rare piece.

Courtesy Henry Francis duPont Winterthur Museum

221. MINIATURE SIDEBOARD

H 6″ x W 8½″
New England, *c.* 1820–1830, Mahogany

The top of this miniature sideboard has square edges which conform to the shape of the case. Bands of complex inlay decorate the vertical edge of the top. Two deep drawers flank one shallow drawer; each deep drawer is divided into two simulated drawers by bands of inlay. The skirt is a half-circle. The center section is divided by the tops of the four legs. From the top to the bottom of the case the legs are square in section and are outlined by two wide bands of light colored wood. Below the case, the legs are disc turned and taper sharply to narrow ankles above large circular spade feet. (See Miller, *American Antique Furniture, A Book for Amateurs,* ex. 986.)

Courtesy Mr. Philip Hammerslaugh

222. MINIATURE SIDEBOARD

H 11¾″ x W 21½″ x D 11½″
America, *c.* 1800, Mahogany, Mahogany veneer

Deep straight edges that are decorated with a line of string inlay complete the top of this sideboard. The six drawers, outlined by a fine line of contrasting light wood, are separated by the four front legs. Surrounding the pulls on the upper drawers are oval bands of inlay consisting of two light lines of string inlay flanking a wider line of dark wood. Similar bands surround the pulls on the lower drawers, but their shape is rectangular with notched corners. The straight skirt is decorated by three thin lines of light colored string inlay separated by two wider lines of darker wood. The legs are short and stumpy, a fault which is disguised by the sharply tapered sides of the four front legs. The legs are decorated by rectangular light string inlay.

Courtesy Yale University Art Gallery
Mabel Brady Garvan Collection

223. MINIATURE SIDEBOARD

H 12½″ x W 20¼″ x D 7¾″
New England, c. 1820, Mahogany; Poplar and Pine (secondary)

The straight edged top of this sideboard conforms to the extended front of the center of the carcass. Across the top is a row of five drawers with beaded edges. The veneering on all the drawers and doors is of superb quality. Miniature desk interior brass pulls adorn the drawers. The skirt is outlined with a band of rope inlay. (See Montgomery, *American Furniture, The Federal Period, 1788–1825*, ex. 17.) A band of this same inlay crosses the front of each of the four front legs. All six legs are daintily turned in the Sheraton fashion. In each of the outside lower drawers flanking the center cupboard, are four fitted places for bottles. This sideboard of magnificent quality was done with the utmost care.

Courtesy Wadsworth Atheneum

SETTLES
&
SETTEES

224. MINIATURE SETTLE

H 8" x W 9⅛" x D 3"
England, *c.* 1650, Oak

This chip-carved miniature settle is of wainscot construction. (See Edwards, *The Shorter Dictionary of English Furniture,* ex. 6.) The three panel back is outlined with chip-carved patterns on the stiles and diamond shaped chip-carved patterns in the center of each sunken panel. The stiles continue to the floor as simple feet. The arms are similar to wainscot chair arms, but are supported by spiral supports which, after their juncture with the seat, become square in section and descend to form simple front feet. (See Edwards, ex. 33.) Below the solid seat is a group of four chip-carved sunken panels separated by vertical stiles with chip-carving. The ends of the seat contain flat recessed panels. The seat opens to give the settle an extra use. A standard piece of furniture of this type could be considerably earlier than this miniature, but after 1650 the arms are more likely to be open. (See Edwards, exx. 13–18, 30, and pp. 118–120.)

Courtesy Mr. and Mrs. Philip Parker

225. CHILD'S COMB-BACK WINDSOR SETTEE

H 27½″ x W 31¼″ x D 14½″
America, 1770, Maple, Hickory

Children's Windsor benches with plank seats and late Sheraton bamboo turnings are fairly common. A child's settee with vase turnings is rare. The serpentine crest rail of this settee is flanked by uncarved ears and is supported by fourteen long spindles that pierce the continuous arm and descend into the seat. The arm, a bent, rectangular board, may have had applied arm rests at one time. The boldly turned arm supports match the turnings on the legs. The thick seat, rounded in front and slightly hollowed for comfort, is supported by six superbly vase turned legs. This settee would be sturdier and more conventional in construction if it had stretchers. Traces of black paint remain.

Courtesy Henry Francis duPont Winterthur Museum

226. MINIATURE SETTEE

America, 19th century, Pine

This primitive miniature settee is made from nailed boards. Except that the back has a more carefully designed and cut profile, this piece is similar to No. 227. The sides exhibit boot jack ends. (See Nutting, *Furniture Treasury*, exx. 2488, 2490, 2491, 2495, 2511.)

Courtesy Wadsworth Atheneum

227. MINIATURE SETTEE

H 19″ x W 20″ x D 9½″
America, Mid 19th century, Poplar

Solid nailed boards were used in the construction of this primitive settee. The back rises to a flat top pierced by an elongated cutout oval. Each side and arm support is made from one board which terminates in crude boot jack ends. A horizontal piece of wood nailed to the top of each arm support forms each arm. A vertical, but slightly rounded board, supports the seat. This settee is very similar to Nos. 38, 39 and 226.

Courtesy Mrs. Herbert F. Schiffer

228. DOLL'S SETTEE EN SUITE WITH DOLL'S CHAIRS

H 8" x W 17¼" x D 6½"
United States, 1810–1840, Black with gold decoration

In order to show to best advantage the decoration which gives them so much of their interest, this miniature fancy Sheraton settee and chairs have wide crest rails. Stiles which show a strong empire influence support the crest rails. (See Lee, *The Ornamented Chair*, p. 88, 89, 100.) The arms on the settee curve downward and are supported by boldly turned supports. The seat, a frame covered by rushing with an additional half-turned member across the front, is supported by square back legs and crisply turned front legs that taper to ball feet. (See Lee, *The Ornamented Chair*, ex. 49.) The legs are strengthened by box stretchers; the back and side stretchers are simple cylinders, while the front stretchers are exquisitely turned. The black background is decorated by gold flowers on the crest rail, gold stripes on the stiles and splats, and gold stripes and leaves in the rectangle at the center of the settee seat rail. The two chairs are similarly decorated, but their center rectangles are empty. These brilliantly conceived and executed pieces of Sheraton miniature furniture support the theory that much miniature was made in sets.

Courtesy Henry Francis duPont Winterthur Museum

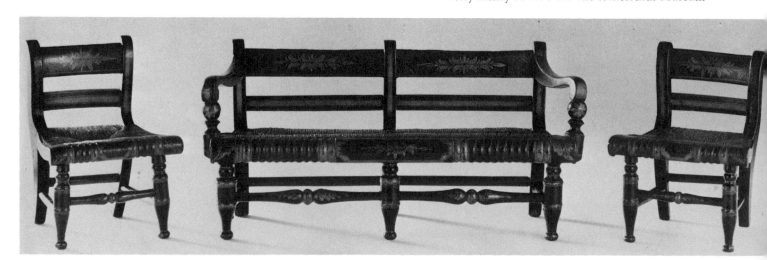

229. DOLL'S MINIATURE SETTEE

H 15¼" x W 24¾" x D 8⅞"
Pennsylvania or Baltimore, c. 1820–1840, Poplar frame,
Pine seat, Red paint with black and gold decoration

An elaborate scroll rises above the center of the crest rail which is supported by four crisply cut and turned stiles. (See Lee, *The Ornamented Chair*, exx. 43–48.) The arms which curve downward are supported by a small turned spindle and by heavily turned arm supports similar to the stiles. The wood frame seat is covered with upholstery which is secured by a beige and green woven tape and nails around the edges. There are eight legs; the back ones are simple spindles which taper below the stretcher and project backward to give the settee a pleasing stance. The boldly turned front legs are strengthened by turned front stretchers. (See Lee, *The Ornamented Chair*, ex. 35.) Simple turned spindle stretchers connect the front and back legs. Gold leaf representations of squirrels and a song book decorate the crest rail; gold balls embellish the turnings. (See *Baltimore Painted Furniture 1800–1840*, p. 13.)

Courtesy Henry Francis duPont Winterthur Museum

230. MINIATURE SHERATON PLANK SEAT BENCH

H 17" x W 27" x D 8½" (seat height 8")
America, c. 1840, Poplar seat, Original green paint, Stenciled decoration, Yellow stripes on seat and legs

The original stenciled design ornaments the crest rail of this bench which is curved and scalloped. The crest rail is supported by three turned spindles, considerably smaller in diameter at the top than at the bottom. The spindles are connected by a narrow rectangular splat. Just below the point at which the stiles pierce the crest rail, the curved arm supports join the two outside stiles and continue forward to terminate in simple outlined scrolls. A spindle, decorated by two disc turnings, supports each arm. The seat which curves downward at the front edge is supported by six well raked legs connected by stretchers. The front legs are decorated by four turned discs, just above their juncture with the stretchers. The back legs are simple spindles which widen in the center and become narrower just before they reach the floor.

Courtesy Mrs. J. Austin duPont

SOFAS

231. MINIATURE SOFA

H 10" x W 9½" x L 19½"
New York (?), c. 1820, Mahogany

The wood of the carved scrolled arms of this sofa is exposed. The seat rail, made of half-round curved mahogany, is also exposed. Four carved animal pad feet support this sofa. Carved wings serve as knee blocks and supports. The upholstery which may be original is made from a paisley shawl.

232. MINIATURE SOFA

H 15" x W 31⅜"
America, possibly New York, c. 1815–1840, Mahogany veneer on cherry

This beautifully proportioned and exquisitely carved empire sofa is crowned by a rounded crest rail which terminates in carved rosettes at each end. The back which has exposed edges is padded with upholstery material held down by a row of decorative tack heads. The upholstery on the scrolled arm is secured in the same manner. The back curves downward and then upward to join the top of the cantered scrolled arms. The front of the seat rail and the front of the arms are exposed wood. Eagles' heads, turned toward the center, and blocks of carved eagles' wings and lions' feet support the sofa.

Courtesy Yale University Art Gallery
Mabel Brady Garvan Collection

233. CHILD'S EMPIRE SOFA

L 54"
Albany or Boston, *c.* 1820, Mahogany

The back of this Grecian couch is bordered by exposed mahogany, carved in the form of a horn of plenty spilling forth its contents. The same carving ornaments the arm supports. The carved wings that act as supports for the seat rail and the crisply carved paw feet are partially obscured by the horn of plenty. The front of the exposed mahogany seat rail is half-round. Though it is of far greater quality throughout, this sofa is similar to No. 232.

Courtesy Peter Hill

234. CLOSE PAIR MINIATURE STOOLS

H 4½" x W 7" x D 5"
H 5" x W 7¾" x D 5¾"
England, *c.* 1780, Mahogany, Pine (secondary)

Carved shells decorate the knees of these extremely rare stools which are supported by cabriole legs and scroll feet. It is possible that they are copied after Sheraton furniture in the French taste.

Courtesy Mrs. J. Austin duPont

235. DOLL'S STOOL

H 2½" x W 4¾" x D 2¾"
Voegler, Pennsylvania, 1830, Mahogany

The top cushion of this stool is supported by deep cove moulded sides that taper inward and descend to a reverse moulded base.

Courtesy Chester County Historical Society

TABLES

237. MINIATURE BANQUET TABLE

H 7⅛″ x W 13½″ x D 13⅜″ (Extended length 24¼″)
England, *c.* 1830, Mahogany

This rectangular banquet table exhibits a moulded top fastened at the ends. The ends which may be pulled apart are connected by a series of slides. Leaves may be added in the center. A beaded edge ornaments the skirt which is supported by turned legs and the original brass casters.

Courtesy Herbert Schiffer Antiques

236. MINIATURE DINING TABLE

236

H 7½″ x L (closed) 16″ x L (open) 33″
New England, *c.* 1810, Striped Maple, Tulip Poplar (secondary)

When closed, this table suggests a half-round card table with extra legs. The rounded edge top is doubled and skirted by bold vertically striped maple. The legs are turned. When the top is folded back, the ends can be pulled apart and extra leaves, supported by an ingenious group of slides, may be added. This charming piece of miniature furniture is a diminutive form of a rare type of large table. It is a mechanical masterpiece and is very possibly a unique form of American miniature furniture.

Courtesy Israel Sack, Inc.

DETAIL NO. 236

237   DETAIL NO. 237

238. DOLL'S POOL TABLE

H 5½″ x W 19½″ x D 11½″
England, *c.* 1800, Mahogany

Rounded edges which are repeated at the bottom of the skirt are applied to the top of this extremely rare pool table. The frame carries the baize covered top and is supported by turned legs. The pockets and balls are period.

Courtesy Mrs. J. Austin duPont

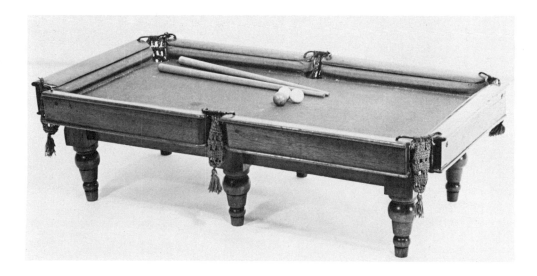

239. MINIATURE TILT-TOP TABLE

H 11″ x W 11″ x D 10¾″
England or America, *c.* 1760, Mahogany

A delicate pedestal, decorated by ring turnings and rising from an urn carved with swirls, supports the top of this tilt-top table. (See Downs, *American Furniture, Queen Anne and Chippendale Periods,* ex. 284.) Many such swirl carved urn stands have been attributed to Newport, Rhode Island; they were also made in England. The cabriole legs terminate in heavily shod pad feet.

Courtesy Mr. and Mrs. Theodore Kapnek

240. MINIATURE SERPENTINE TILT-TOP TABLE

H 12″ x W 12″ x D 12″
Massachusetts, *c.* 1780, Mahogany

A ring and vase turned pillar supports the deeply serpentined top of this table. The three cabriole legs terminate in deep pad feet. The legs and the bottom of the pedestal are notched. (See Randall, *American Furniture in the Museum of Fine Arts,* ex. 106.) Because of their strong similarities, this example and example 106 may have come from the same shop—that of Jonathan Grave.

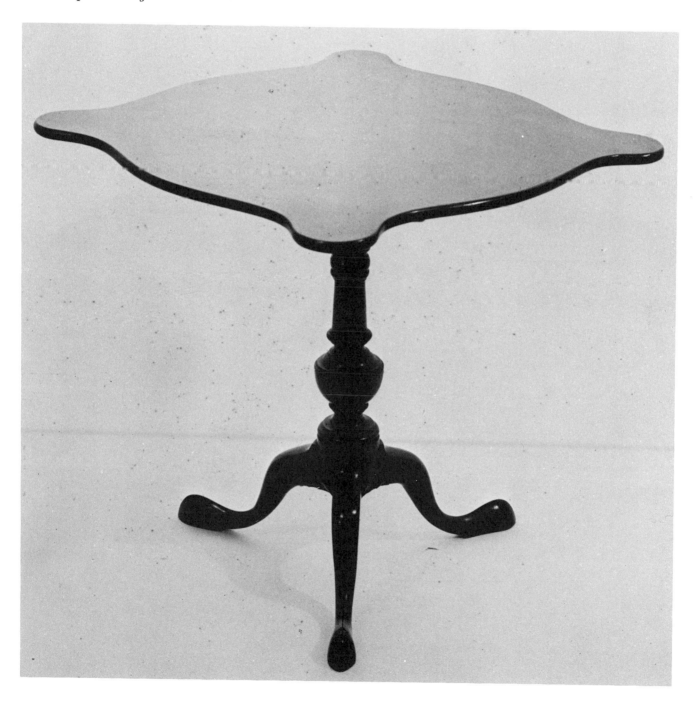

241. MINIATURE HEPPLEWHITE CANDLESTAND

H 9½" x W 6" x D 6"
New Bedford, Massachusetts, *c.* 1800, Mahogany and Maple

The elongated octagonal top of this candlestand is decorated with a border of veneer. Solid wood lies between this border and the inlaid border of bird's eye maple triangles. The center of the top is decorated by a bird's eye maple oval and a primitive star pattern. Three gracefully tapered spider legs support the simply turned pedestal.

242. MINIATURE CARD TABLE

H 6⅞" x W 9⅝" x D 9⅜"
England, *c.* 1770, Mahogany

This card table exhibits a rectangular mahogany double top with a half-round edge. The hinges are not placed as they would be on a full scale table. Rectangular patterns suggesting two small drawers decorate the straight skirt. In the center of each simulated drawer is a picture ring brass pull. Tapered square legs, slightly heavier in section than is desirable, support the table. One leg swings back to support the top when it is open.

Courtesy Victoria and Albert Museum

243. DOLL'S CARD TABLE

H 5″ x W 9⅛″ x D 4½″
America, *c.* 1830, Mahogany

A rectangular top with slightly rounded corners and miniature card table hinges adorns this table. The top turns to the side and rests on the straight skirt. This method was frequently used by Duncan Phyfe and other New York cabinetmakers. The skirt is decorated at its edge with an applied half-round moulding which curves upward into a carved applied flower. The pedestal, turned at the top and carved into slightly elongated beading, rests on a section with four concave areas cut out between the corners. These turreted corners are supported by carved feet similar to the base of the pedestal.

Courtesy Mr. Philip Hammerslaugh

DETAIL NO. 243

239

244. DOLL'S DRESSING TABLE

H 5¾" x W 6½" x D 4½"
England, Late 17th century, Oak with Walnut veneer

The top of this William and Mary lowboy is bordered by a band of diagonally grained veneer one quarter inch in from the edge. The deeply moulded edge has a noticeable overhang. The case contains one drawer with plain edges and two drop pulls. Surrounding the drawer is an applied double-arch moulding. The veneered drawer has a band of diagonally placed inlay at its edge. The walnut veneer on the case is vertically grained. Two concave curves, outlined with applied bead moulding, form the skirt. At the center of the sides and at the front are capped drops which are repeated above the four legs. Each leg is ring and vase turned. From the top, the legs are ornamented by ring, vase, disc and trumpet turnings. The cross stretchers have French curves that complement the curves of the skirt. Below the stretchers are disc turnings and ball feet.

Courtesy Victoria and Albert Museum

245. MINIATURE DRESSING TABLE

H 15½" x W 20¾" x D 11½"
Massachusetts, 1740–1760, Walnut and Maple, White Pin(e) (secondary)

This dressing table has a rectangular top with moulded edge and an exceptionally large overhang. Except for the center skirt and the center drawe(r) which have a concave semi-circular block, the cas(e) is rectangular. The blocked rectangular cent(er) drawer is flanked by two straight drawers. All thre(e) drawers have lipped edges and small brass pull(s). The skirt is decorated with French curves and tw(o)

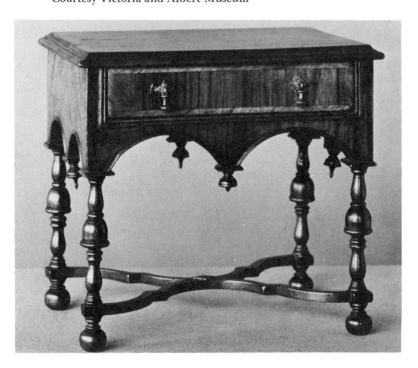

ndants; at one time drops probably hung below
em. The cabriole legs are flanked by curved knee
ocks and taper through delicate ankles to slightly
od flat pad feet. (Note this piece has a tradition
ownership in the Emerson family of Concord,
assachusetts.)

urtesy Henry Francis duPont Winterthur Museum

246. MINIATURE DRESSING TABLE

H 9″ x W 11⅞″ x D 7¾″
New England, c. 1725–1750, Mahogany, White Pine (secondary)

The case of this dressing table contains one long
drawer above three shorter drawers. The center
drawer is decorated by an intaglio carved fan. The
lipped drawers have interior desk pulls. Two drops
with finials ornament the skirt which is shaped
with French curves. Boldly shaped cabriole legs,
flanked at the top by curved glue blocks, support
the case. The sharply kneed legs descend through
fine ankles to flat pad feet. (See Downs, *American
Furniture, Queen Anne and Chippendale Periods*,
ex. 186). Although these dressing tables are called
lowboys today, the term does not occur in the 18th
or early 19th century wills, deeds or inventories of
Chester County, Pennsylvania. Lowboy is a term
that came into antique descriptions in the last
quarter of the 19th century with the revived interest in 18th century furniture.

Courtesy Henry Francis duPont Winterthur Museum

241

247. DOLL'S GATELEG TABLE

H 5½" x W 7¼"
England, *c.* 1720, Oak

Each drop leaf of this William and Mary hexagonal table is supported by two gates. This is an unusual occurrence on such a small piece. The legs, vase and ring turned, terminate in ball feet with small spindle extensions. The stretchers are rectangular in section.

Courtesy Mrs. J. Austin duPont

248. DOLL'S DROP LEAF TABLE

H 7¼" x W 9⅞" x D 10"
England, *c.* 1720, Oak

Queen Anne round drop leaf tables are rare in miniature furniture. When the leaves are down, the two swing legs of this table fit tightly into the frame as do the legs of standard size gateleg tables. The table stands on four boldly curved cabriole legs that terminate in shod pad feet.

Courtesy Mr. and Mrs. Philip Parker

249. MINIATURE PEMBROKE TABLE

H 10" x W 14½" x D 9⅝"
New England, *c.* 1810, Maple and Mahogany

This Pembroke table has a rectangular top and drop leaves with rounded corners. There is a simple butt joint between the leaves and the top. The hinges are original. Now lost, slides once came out from under the top to support the leaves. The table stands on four square legs that taper gently to the floor.

Courtesy Herbert Schiffer Antiques

250. MINIATURE PEMBROKE TABLE

H 11½″ x W 15″ x D (closed) 8″, (open) 22″
America, *c.* 1830, Cherry, Pine (secondary)

A rectangular top with notched corners covers this table which contains a plain nailed drawer. Except for decorative ring turning embellishments, the legs descend as cylinders and terminate in ball feet. Wood slides open to support the leaves of this table.

Courtesy Mrs. J. Austin duPont

250

251. MINIATURE DUMB WAITER

H 12″ x W 5″
England, *c.* 1760, Mahogany

Three graduated round table tops with moulded dish rims complete this miniature dumb waiter. The cylindrical pedestal between the tables is decorated by vase shaped ring turnings. Below the bottom table, the pedestal, decorated by a ball and several ring turnings, is supported by three graceful cabriole legs terminating in dophin feet. Each top turns separately.

Courtesy Victoria and Albert Museum

252. CHILD'S TABLE

H 21¼" x W 22¼" x D 16½"
New England, *c.* 1790, Walnut, Pine (secondary)

This table has a beautifully moulded rim edge; it is possible that it may have been positioned lower where it would not have presented the tray top effect it gives today. A wooden knob adorns the drawer which is dovetailed in front. The legs which are turned terminate in disc feet.

Courtesy Henry Francis duPont Winterthur Museum

253. MINIATURE TABLE

H 17½" x W 11" x D 11¼"
New England, *c.* 1800–1820, Maple and Mahogany; Poplar (secondary)

The straight edged square top of this table exhibits a great deal of overhang. A simple wooden knob is attached to the drawer. Directly below the drawer, the legs are turned with ring turnings and a bulbous section. They continue as simple spindles and descend to a ring turning and a bulbous tapered foot.

Courtesy Henry Francis duPont Winterthur Museum

254. MINIATURE NIGHT TABLE

H 14" x W 11¼" x D 6½"
America, *c.* 1800, Mahogany veneer on Poplar, Poplar (secondary)

A rounded edge borders this table's rectangular top with rounded corners. The two drawers are placed above each other in a case supported by a turned pedestal on four legs. The drawers have brass knobs and are veneered with a good choice of mahogany.

Courtesy Mrs. J. Austin duPont

255. DOLL'S CENTER TABLE

H 6⅜" x W 9¾" x D 7¼"
England, *c.* 1760, Mahogany

A thick rectangular top with straight edges covers this center table. The top is edged by a large ogee moulding which is repeated on a smaller scale around the skirt. Large square legs, chamfered on the inside corners, support the table. The boldness of the legs and the vigor of the top moulding combine to make this a most attractive miniature.

Courtesy Mr. and Mrs. Philip Parker

256. DOLL'S PIER OR SERVING TABLE

H 10" x W 14½" x D 9⅝"
England, *c.* 1800, Mahogany

The straight edged rectangular top of this serving table has a noticeable overhang. The straight skirt is recessed. Prominent square blocks which jut in front of the skirt continue into the legs. They taper from ring turnings through double ring turned cuffs and terminate in round spade feet.

Courtesy Herbert Schiffer Antiques

257. CHILD'S PIER TABLE

H 23″ x W 23″ x D 11″
America, probably Salem, Mass., c. 1790, Walnut, holly, and ebony inlay, Poplar (secondary)

The top of this half-round pier table is surrounded by a cove moulding. This moulding is similar to those seen on many of the full scale Hepplewhite card tables. The lower edge of the skirt is ornamented with five lines of contrasting inlay which alternate between light and dark. The rectangular legs which taper sharply to very small feet are interrupted by inlaid cuffs.

Courtesy Mrs. J. Austin duPont

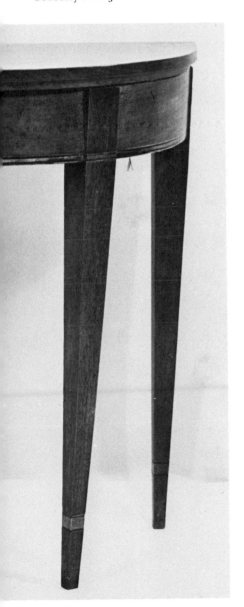

258. MINIATURE PIER TABLE

H 7¼″ x W 9″ x D 4⅝″
England, c. 1780, Mahogany, Veneered skirting

One of a pair of rare D end transitional Chippendale to Hepplewhite miniature pier tables, this beautiful table has rounded corners. The double moulding at the top edge is repeated at the bottom edge of the skirt. Beautiful mahogany veneer covers the skirt.

Courtesy Mr. and Mrs. Philip Parker

247

259. MINIATURE MARBLE TOP PIER TABLE

H 9½″ x W 9⅞″ x D 6″
F. T. Johnson, America, 1834, Mahogany, Maple inlay,
Marble top, Mirrored back

Beneath the marble top of this table is a deep complicated moulding supported by the straight frame which surrounds the mirrored back. The front legs are carved scrolls and are ornamented by applied carved rosettes. The mirror and the front legs rest on a deep plinth with turreted supports for the scrolls. The base stands on four feet turned in a series of three graduated discs. The two front feet are embellished by a carved spray of leaves on the largest disc. This table is a masterpiece of cabinetwork, a successful example of empire design, and a very important documentary piece because it is dated and signed. The signature is:
Made and presented by: F. T. Johnson
Cabinet Maker
43 Southport below Almon
March 29, 1834

Courtesy Greenfield Village and Henry Ford Museum

248

260. MINIATURE MARBLE TOPPED PIER TABLE

H 7½" x W 12½" x D 5"
Philadelphia, c. 1836, Mahogany, Mahogany veneer

Supported by a broad, complex, moulded skirt, the top is a rectangular slab of marble with straight edges and some overhang. The skirt is supported by carved, scrolled legs in front and by the frame that contains the mirrored back. The frame and the legs rest on a deep plinth. Between the base of the two front legs, the plinth has a deeply cut concave shape.

Courtesy Chester County Historical Society

261. DOLL'S TRAY-ON-FOLDING-STAND

H 5¾" x W 5¾" x D 4⅛"
Voegler, Philadelphia, 1836, Mahogany

This is the only American miniature tray we have seen. The tray-on-stand is a form that is principally English. A few Dutch miniatures do exist; one can be seen in the Reich Museum in Amsterdam. This particular tray exhibits dovetailed corners and sides cut out for hand holds. The back and sides are higher than the front. A turned folding base supports the tray.

Courtesy Chester County Historical Society

262

262. MINIATURE TAVERN TABLE

H 11¾″ x W 11″ x D 9″
America, *c.* 1710, Walnut

An oval top with a rounded edge completes this tavern table. The boldly scalloped skirt rests on raked legs decorated with ring turnings at the top and at the bottom. The legs are square in section at their juncture with the stretchers, are turned again, and terminate in ball feet. A bead is cut in the two upper edges and in the lower outside edges of the stretchers.

Courtesy Mrs. J. Austin duPont

263. DOLL'S TAVERN (CRICKET) TABLE

H 8⅝″ x D 7⅞″
England, *c.* 1690, Oak

The rounded edge top of this cricket table is supported by three vase turned legs terminating in elongated ball feet. An unadorned triangular skirt connects the legs which are strengthened by simple stretchers.

Courtesy Mr. Philip Parker

264. CHILD'S TAVERN TABLE

H 19″ x W 26¾″ x D 19½″
America, c. 1770, Pine, Poplar (secondary)

This tavern table has a rectangular breadboard top. A wooden knob is attached to the drawer which is carefully dovetailed. The skirt and sides are plain. The four vase and disc turned legs have no rake, are strengthened by box stretchers and terminate in ball feet which have been restored. The surface has a coat of blue paint over traces of old red paint.

Courtesy Herbert Schiffer Antiques

265. DOLL'S PORRINGER TOP TEA TABLE

H 8⅜″ x W 13″ x D 8″
New England, *c.* 1740, Mahogany

This miniature tea table is a great rarity. The thick, round edged top has porringer corners. Opposing pairs of French curves form brackets for the straight skirt. At their juncture with the skirt, the legs are square in section; below that juncture they become round in section and taper gracefully to ankles which terminate in shod pad feet. (For standard size examples see Nutting. *Furniture Treasury,* ex. 885.)

Courtesy Mr. and Mrs. Robert Lee Gill

266. DOLL'S TEA TABLE

H 7″ x W 10¾″ x D 7″
England, *c.* 1730, Mahogany

Reverse curves flank the rounded corners of this tea table. The serpentine edge of the top is echoed in the serpentine skirt which exhibits a scrolled and cyma curved lower edge. At the sides is a short reverse curve. The cabriole legs terminate in shod pad feet.

Courtesy Mr. and Mrs. Theodore Kapnek

267. DOLL'S TEA TABLE

H 6½″ x W 7¾″ x D 5¾″
England, *c.* 1730, Mahogany

This miniature tea table has a rectangular top bordered by raised applied moulding. A series of cyma and ogee curves embellishes the skirt. This feature is carried further in the cyma curved glue blocks which flank the legs. The cabriole legs descend through delicate ankles to terminate in bold pad feet.

Courtesy Mrs. J. Austin duPont

268. MINIATURE WAKE TABLE

H 4¼″ x W (closed) 3¼″ x L 22″ (Each leaf 3⅜″ wide)
Ireland, *c.* 1760, Mahogany

The elongated oval top of this table is supported by eight legs. The four fixed legs and the four swing legs are square in section and taper as they descend to the floor. Most full scale wake tables have straight or cabriole legs.

Courtesy Mr. Philip Parker

DETAIL NO. 268

269. DOLL'S BASIN STAND

H 7⅜" x W 3" x D 3¾"
England, c. 1760, Mahogany

Four square beaded legs support the two shelves of this basin stand. The top shelf which is pierced to receive a basin is surrounded by an applied moulding and a semi-curved skirt below. Another skirt, conforming in shape to the one above, surrounds the second shelf which probably held a ewer. To lighten the design, the solid stretcher is cut back between the legs in half-circle curves. When turned over, this piece shows its authenticity and handmade quality to an unusual degree.

Courtesy Victoria and Albert Museum

270

270. MINIATURE WASHSTAND

H 16⅞" x W 8" x D 8"
England, c. 1760, Mahogany

Because it has been converted into a night table, the top of this washstand is removable. Below this newer top, is the original top which is pierced to receive a washbasin. A scalloped skirt ornaments the top shelf. Except for chamfered corners on the interior side, the four straight Chippendale legs are square in section. Between the top shelf and the center section, which contains a drawer, lamb's-tongues embellish the chamfered corners. The drawer is edged by a scratch bead and has two stirrup pulls. Cross stretchers strengthen the legs.

Courtesy Mr. Philip Parker

271. DOLL'S WASHSTAND

H 9¾" x W 5¼" x D 5¼"
England, c. 1740, Mahogany

Three holes pierce the top of this washstand which retains its original finish. The stand is supported by four legs, chamfered on the inside corners as they descend to the drawer. Below the drawer which has a brass knob, the legs taper to the floor.

Courtesy Mr. Philip Parker

272. CHILD'S CORNER WASHSTAND

H 26½″ x W 11¼″ x D 8″
England, c. 1780, Mahogany

This corner washstand is crested by two boards which rise to an arch at the back corner. The top shelf is a quarter-round triangle pierced by three holes. The middle shelf contains three drawers with pressed brass knobs; the bottom shelf has a serpentine front edge. Three legs support this washstand; the two front legs flare out boldly to suggest French feet.

Courtesy Mr. Philip Parker

273. MINIATURE WASHSTAND

H 14¾" x W 7⅜" x 7⅜"
New England, 1810, Maple, Cherry, White Pine and Walnut

A top, protected by a nailed back and sides rising above the top, completes this washstand. The top which has a rounded front edge is pierced to receive a washbasin. The skirt is deep and straight. The legs which alternate from being square in section to being ring turned descend to bulbous turned cuffs above tapered spindles. The single drawer has straight edges and a wooden knob. An important feature of this piece is the carefully selected striped maple used throughout.

Courtesy Yale University Art Gallery
Mabel Brady Garvan Collection

273

274. DOLL'S NIGHTSTAND

H 8" x W 6¼" x D 5⅛"
Voegler, Philadelphia, 1836, Mahogany, Poplar (secondary)

A wooden gallery on the back and sides crowns the top of this nightstand. The half-round drawer, vertical in section, is decorated by a glass knob. The turned legs, strengthened by rectangular stretchers, are further connected by a shelf with a scalloped front edge. The drawer is of nailed construction.

Courtesy Chester County Historical Society

275. DOLL'S WINE TABLE

H 8½" x D 5"
England, c. 1750, Mahogany

The dish top of this table rests on a pedestal supported by three cabriole legs on shod feet. The pedestal exhibits an urn turning and an unusual concave turning. The smallness of the top in proportion to the spread of the legs indicates that this is a wine table. Because wine tables were designed to hold only a decanter and a few glasses, they were made with small tops. Widely spread legs were necessary to give the table stability.

Courtesy Mrs. J. Austin duPont

275

BIBLIOGRAPHY

Andrews, Edward, and Andrews, Faith. *Shaker Furniture*. New York: Dover Publications, Inc., 1950.

Bailey, Rosalie F. *Pre-Revolutionary Dutch Houses and Families in Northern New Jersey and Southern New York*. New York: Dover Publications, Inc., 1968.

Baltimore Museum of Art. *Baltimore Painted Furniture 1800–1840*. Baltimore: The Baltimore Museum of Art, 1972.

Bjerkoe, Ethel Hall. *The Cabinet Makers of America*. Garden City, New York: Doubleday and Company, 1957.

Chippendale, Thomas. *The Gentleman and Cabinet Maker's Director*. London: Becket & Hondt, 1754.

Culff, Robert. *The World of Toys*. Feltham, Middlesex, England: The Hamlyn House Publishing Group Limited, 1969.

Davidson, Marshall B. *The American Heritage History of Colonial Antiques*. New York: American Heritage Pub. Co., Inc., 1967.

Downs, Joseph. *American Furniture, Queen Anne and Chippendale Periods in the Henry Francis duPont Winterthur Museum*. New York: MacMillan Co., 1952.

Edwards, Ralph. *The Shorter Dictionary of English Furniture*. London: Country Life Limited, 1964.

Grandjean, Serge. *Empire Furniture*. New York: Taplinger Pub. Co., 1966.

Hope, Thomas. *Household Furniture and Interior Decoration, Executed from Designs by Thomas Hope*. London: Longman, Hurst, Rees and Orme, 1807.

Horner, William M., Jr. *Blue Book, Philadelphia Furniture, William Penn to George Washington*. Philadelphia: Privately Printed, 1935.

Kirk, John T. *Early American Furniture*. New York: Alfred A. Knopf, 1970.

Lee, Zilla Rider. *The Ornamented Chair, Its Development in America (1700–1890)*. Rutland, Vermont: Charles E. Tuttle Co., 1960.

Lichten, Frances. *Folk Art of Rural Pennsylvania*. New York: Charles Scribner's Sons, New York, 1946.

Miller, Edgar C., Jr. *American Antique Furniture, A Book for Amateurs.* New York: M. Barrows & Co., Inc., 1937.

Montgomery, Charles. *American Furniture, The Federal Period, 1788–1825.* New York: The Viking Press, 1966.

Newark Museum. *Classical America, 1815–1845.* Newark, New Jersey: The Newark Museum, 1963.

Nutting, Wallace. *Furniture of the Pilgrim Century.* New York: Dover Publications, Inc., 1965.

————. *Furniture Treasury.* New York: The MacMillan Co., 1954.

Ormsbee, Thomas. *The Windsor Chair.* New York: Hearthside Press, 1962.

Palmer, Brooks. *The Book of American Clocks.* New York: The MacMillan Co., 1956.

Randall, Richard. *American Furniture in the Museum of Fine Arts.* Boston: Museum of Fine Arts, 1956.

Sack, Albert. *Fine Points of Furniture: Early American.* New York: Crown Publishers, Inc., 1950.

Schiffer, Margaret B. *Furniture and Its Makers of Chester County, Pennsylvania.* Philadelphia: University of Pennsylvania Press, 1966.

Stoudt, John Joseph. *Early Pennsylvania Arts and Crafts.* New York: A. S. Barnes & Co., 1964.

Strange, T. A. *English Furniture, Decoration, Woodwork and Allied Arts.* London: Strange, N.D.

Victoria and Albert Museum. *Dolls' Houses.* London: Her Majesty's Stationery Office, 1960.

Wadsworth Atheneum. *Connecticut Furniture of the 17th and 19th Century, Catalogue.* Hartford: Wadsworth Atheneum, 1967.

Ward, J. D. U. "Early English Baby Chairs." *Antiques Magazine,* October 1941, p. 224.

Wills, Geoffrey. *English Looking Glasses 1670–1820.* London: Country Life, Limited, 1965.

GLOSSARY

This glossary is offered as a guide to technical references in this book. It is not our intention to cover the nomenclature of all antique furniture subjects. Please consult the bibliography for additional references.

ACANTHUS An ornamentation carved to resemble the acanthus leaves, for use on furniture and in architecture

BAIL A drawer pull of curved design, secured by bolts, backed by a decorative plate, and usually made of brass

BAIZE A fabric, usually woolen, dyed and with a coarse, long-napped consistency

BALL FOOT A turned, rounded foot on furniture

Ball foot

BALL TURNING See TURNING

BALUSTER A banister; an upright support of a rail, usually of a turned and vase-shaped design

BATTEN A strip of wood used for re-enforcement, particularly in joining two wide boards

BATWING BRASS Brass drawer pulls and escutcheons which resemble a bat's wings

Batwing brass

BEAD MOULDING See MOULDING

BOLECTION A moulding with a bold, prominent, projecting surface; one use of which is the framing and division of panel sections

BONNET-TOP A pediment of broken-scroll design, which forms a hood topping tall case furniture

BOSS A knoblike ornament used as decoration; a stud

BOX STRETCHER See STRETCHER

BRACKET FOOT A foot with mitered corners and unjoined sides that are often scrolled; characteristic of case furniture

Bracket foot

BREWSTER CHAIR A chair identified by turned posts and ornamented spindles which appear on the back, and below the seat and arms; a form of Pilgrim chair

CABOCHON A carved ornament, that surmounts a decorative motif, which can be either spherical or oval, convex or concave

CANT A type of bevel or chamfer

CAPITAL The uppermost section of a column or pilaster which crowns the shaft and supports the entablature

CHAMFER The surface formed by smoothing, planing, or cutting away an angle or an edge

CHIP CARVING A simple form of decorative carving, popular during the Middle Ages, in which patterns first prepared with compasses, are then chipped out of wooden surfaces

COCKBEAD MOULDING See MOULDING

CORNICE In architecture, the uppermost horizontal section of an entablature

CRESTING The carved decoration on the top rail of a chair, settee, day bed, or mirror

CROSS STRETCHER See STRETCHER

CYMA In architecture, a section or the moulding of the cornice having a wavy or curved profile; an ogee

DENTILS   A series of small, decorative, rectangular blocks, equally spaced and projecting as under a cornice

DISC TURNING   See TURNING

DOVETAIL   Flaring tenons (resembling a dove's tail) which interlace to form a right-angled joint

EGLOMISE PANEL   A technique of decor that involves any painted glass panel used in furniture, clocks, mirrors, or picture frames

ESCUTCHEON   The shaped surface on which armorial bearings are displayed; also a decorative shield used around a keyhold to protect wood

EWER   A form of wide-mouthed jug

FINIAL   A crowning architectural or design detail used as a terminal ornament

FRENCH FOOT   A bracket foot with an outward curve

FRETWORK   Ornamental openwork or work in relief with a design similar to latticework

GATELEG   Gatelike legs support the drop leaves of the table when open and fold against the frame of the table when closed

GILT   Overlaid with a thin covering of gold, or a substance resembling gold

GOLD LEAF   An extremely thin leaf of gold used for gilding

HIGHBOY   A high chest of drawers set upon a lower case of drawers on tablelike legs.

H STRETCHER   See STRETCHER

INLAY   Decoration attained by setting contrasting materials into the body of a surface

INTAGLIO   An incised design, depressed below the surface of the material; opposed to cameo

JAPANNING   To lacquer or cover with a coat of japan or other varnish having similar properties of hardness and brilliance

LAMB'S-TONGUE   A geometric shape formed by the terminus (resembling a lamb's tongue) of a chamfer

MITER (MITRE)   The diagonal joint in a moulding formed by the two pieces of woodwork intersecting at right angles

MORTISE & TENON   The joining of two pieces of material, usually wood, by the insertion of one piece (the tenon) into the cavity or socket (the mortise) of the other

MOULDING   A decorative band that is obtained by a continuous projection or incision applied to a surface

BEAD   A moulding with a surface consisting of small, round, projecting shapes

COCK BEAD   A projecting moulding that consists of small, half-round sections; usually applied to drawer fronts

OGEE   A moulding having an S-shaped profile

QUARTER-ROUND   An ovolo; the name in both architecture and cabinetmaking for a convex moulding precisely quarter round in section

SCRATCH BEAD   A simulated beading formed by a scratch or continuous indentation along the edge of a board

STEP   A moulding with a cross-section resembling steps

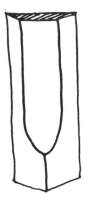

Lamb's-tongue

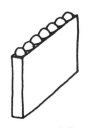

Bead moulding

Ogee moulding

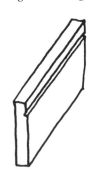

Scratch bead moulding

French foot

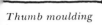
Thumb moulding

THUMB   A convex moulding with a flat curve that resembles the profile of a thumb

OGEE   See CYMA and MOULDING

PATERA   Small carved ornaments either oval or round, used in the decoration of such items as friezes, mirror crestings, and chair splats

PATINA   The surface of woods or metals mellowing, in color or finish, with age or use

PEDIMENT   A triangular feature at the top of, for example, a portico or at the head of, e.g., a cabinet

BROKEN-ARCH   A curved pediment interrupted at the apex

PILASTER   An upright rectangular member, structurally a pier, but architecturally treated as a column

PINNATE LEAVES   Characterized by the division of the leaflets, or primary sections, onto each side of a common leafstalk, or extension of a leafstalk

PLATE RAIL   A primitive flat rail characterized by a raised outer edge

PLINTH   The lowest section of a base, or a block serving as a base for objects such as urns, vases, or statues

QUARTER-ROUND MOULDING   See MOULDING

RING TURNING   See TURNING

SCRATCH BEAD MOULDING   See MOULDING

SERPENTINE   Resembling a serpent or having a winding, turning surface

SLIPPER FOOT   A slender foot, pointed and extended

Slipper foot

SLIP SEAT   Known also as "loose seat;" the separate upholstered wood frame that is let into the framing of the chair seat

SPADE FOOT   A tapered rectangular foot having a spade-shaped profile

SPANDREL   A usually triangular element that is used for decorative purposes in a corner, or corners

SPANISH FOOT   A scroll foot having vertical rib designs within the scroll curve

SPLAT   An upright, single center support of a chair back having flat, thin features

SPOOL TURNING   See TURNING

STEP MOULDING   See MOULDING

STILE   An upright side support in a chair back

STRETCHER   The rungs or crosspieces that connect the legs of chairs and tables, etc.

BOX   The stretchers that connect the legs in an unending continuous line

CROSS   The X-shape, horizontal brace which connects the legs of chairs, tables, and case pieces

H   The stretcher construction in which stretchers from the front to the back leg, on each side, are connected through the middle by the use of a third piece

TESTER   The canopy, either of fabric or wood, over a bed

THUMB MOULDING   See MOULDING

TILL   As used in a cabinet, a secret drawer or tray

Spanish foot

TRESTLE FOOT   Rectangular blocks of wood extending from each side of the end of a table leg in order to provide better stability

TRIFID FOOT   Three-toed; also called a drake foot

TROMPE L'OEIL   Any form of decoration that can deceive or "fool-the-eye" of the beholder

Trifid foot

TRUMPET TURNING   See TURNING

TURNING   An ancient craft of woodworking in which cutting tools are applied to a rotating surface

> BALL   Spherical turnings; usually in a series

> DISC   Turnings which resemble a disc or discus in profile

> RING   Turnings giving the appearance of a flattened ball turning

> SPOOL   A series of bulbous turnings that resemble rows of spools

> TRUMPET   A turned leg having the profile of an upturned trumpet

> VASE   A turning resembling a vase, with a bulbous base beneath a taper shape

VASE TURNING   See TURNING

VOLUTE   An ornament with a spiral or rolled-up conformation

WAINSCOT   The modern designation for the panel back chair; or any chair of solid construction

YOKE   The term applied to the crest rail of a chair back

Ball turning

Disc turning

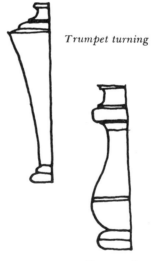

Trumpet turning

Vase turning .

Miniature Antique Furniture has been set in
linotype Baskerville by Cherry Hill Composition
Company with Bulmer foundry display by P-H-P
Graphic Arts Corporation.
Paper is Mountie Publishers Matte made by the
Northwest Paper Company.
The book was printed and bound by the Maple Press.
Cloth is Bolton Buckram made by the
Columbia Mills, Inc.
Design by Fletcher MacNeill.
Jacket and Typographic design by John Anderson.